MW01194198

Freedom FROM FEAR

A Way
Through The Ways
Of Jesus The Christ

FRANCIS W. VANDERWALL

Acadian House
PUBLISHING
LAFAYETTE, LOUISIANA

Library of Congress Catalog Card Number: 99-62093

ISBN: 0-925417-34-3

All scripture quotes used in the author's text were taken from either *The Jerusalem Bible* or *The New Jerusalem Bible*, New York: Doubleday and Co., Inc., 1966 and 1985, respectively.

- ◆ Published by Acadian House Publishing, Lafayette, Louisiana (Edited by Trent Angers; graphic design by Brent Leger)
- ◆ Cover illustration and design by Michelle Marse, Lafayette, Louisiana
- ◆ Inside illustrations by Kenn Kotara, Asheville, North Carolina
- ◆ Poetry by Leo Luke Marcello, Lake Charles, Louisiana
- ◆ Printed by BookCrafters, Fredericksburg, Virginia

A Ring Of Truth

When I first heard that Francis Vanderwall had completed his manuscript titled *Freedom From Fear* and was seeking a publisher, I was only mildly interested.

That interest was heightened, though, when I learned that the book delved into both psychology and theology, that it dealt with fear, shame, guilt, worry, anxiety and the like, and that it used the parables of Jesus as the antidote to these conditions.

I detected a certain ring of truth in this approach even before I read the first page. I also gathered from others that Dr. Vanderwall was eminently qualified to write on this subject, being a counselor, spiritual director, retreat leader, former Jesuit, and a doctor of philosophy in the psychology of religion.

When he came to my office with the manuscript, we talked about the work and the subjects of theology, scripture, psychology and the like. Rather than feeling intimidated by his considerable knowledge of these subjects, I was comfortable talking with him about them and about the potential book he was presenting to me. This is because the message of his manuscript was so germane to the central teachings of Jesus, i.e., that He came to bring salvation and life in abundance.

In the course of this conversation, he made a few observations that struck me as the unmitigated truth. For one thing, he pointed out that Jesus commanded us to love God and to love one another, but that it was virtually impossible to carry out these commandments if we were imprisoned by fear, which is the opposite of love. A person who lives in the clutches of fear is not free to love in a healthy, open manner, if at all. Though love is a most powerful virtue, fear is an insidious enemy which can creep up on us and sap the life and the love out of us – until we identify it, name it for what it is, and find the courage to deal with it. As Ralph Waldo Emerson once wrote: "Do the thing you fear, and the death of fear is certain."

I took the manuscript home and put it next to my reading chair, intending to get to it in a few days, possibly over the weekend. But my curiosity was up and so I started reading it that night. I thought I might read a few paragraphs of the introduction, but that gave way to a page, then two, and before I knew it I was well into the book and it was way past my bedtime. I continued reading and I knew that night that what was in this book had the power to heal, the power to help free people from their fears, just as its title implies.

It struck me how relevant and on-point this work would be to so many people. The thought even crossed my mind, and it continues to cross my mind, that I have never met a person in my entire life (50 years and counting) who would not benefit from reading this book. And I mean this literally. To some, it would be mildly beneficial; to others it could be as important as the air they breathe.

After all, who among us has not been paralyzed by fear at some point in our lives? Who has not experienced guilt or shame or anxiety in levels that tend to cripple us psychologically, for a little while or for a long period of time?

As I continued reading through the manuscript, I realized there was a certain similarity between Dr. Vanderwall's writings and the writings of the late Dr. Norman Vincent Peale, the author of *The Power of Positive Thinking.* Both men's works deal with psychology and theology together, in the same breath. Both works are progressive and represent profound thinking, bringing light to areas of human knowledge that were not so well-illuminated before. Both works are practical, theologically sound and self-empowering – and applicable to the burdens borne by huge numbers of people.

The words in this book ring true in part because they resonate so perfectly with the scriptures that deal with fear, in the Old Testament and in the New. One example is the Twenty-Third Psalm: "...Though I walk through the valley of the shadow of death, I will fear no evil, for you are with me...." Another, written by St. Paul in a letter to Timothy, speaks of one of God's great gifts to us all, in language that is most encouraging: "God has not given us the spirit of fear, but of power and of love and of a sound mind."

Like the Gospels themselves, this book proclaims the Good News of salvation, of freedom from fear and want, and of life in great abundance.

– *Trent Angers,* SFO
Editor

iv

To the Society of Jesus,
with gratitude

Acknowledgments

As I reflect back with gratitude on the many friends who helped me with this book, I single out for particular mention and thanks the following:

Dr. David Duncombe, who directed my studies both at Yale and Berkeley;

Dr. Tom Hart, a friend and meticulous critic both in Berkeley and from Seattle;

Dr. Kevina Keating, CCVI, who challenged me both from San Francisco and Houston;

Kenn Kotara for his insightful and challenging artwork;

Dr. Leo Luke Marcello for his moving poetry;

My parents, Will and Pearl Vanderwall, for their continuing faith in and support of me;

And finally Gloria Judd, without whom the tedious and almost daily computer entries and editing would not have taken place.

Thank you very much!

I must add, however, that I take full responsibility for the book's content and together with my courageous publisher, Trent Angers, trust that it will reach your hearts, wherever you may be.

Contents

Introduction

The enemy of love is fear. Many of our behaviors – religious, economic, social and intellectual – have a common, often hidden, motivator: fear. If we honestly examine our hearts and minds we may be astonished at how much fear we have entrenched within us.

We fear what we do not understand, and we seek accordingly to set up structures (personal, societal and religious) to protect us from fears. For instance, fear of rejection can frequently cause a gentle man to become cold and demanding; a society fearful of an enormous national debt can cut programs for its most helpless members with impunity; a church fearful of losing its control and power over an increasingly educated congregation can revert to dictatorial measures to reassert its control.

Jesus, as well as many of the prophets of the Old Testament, knew the negative consequences of fear. Over and over again they called us to lose our fears, to let go of them and the fallacious security they provide. Fear, in fact, is the first recorded emotion after the fall.

"Where are you?" God calls out to the man. And the man replies, "I heard the sound of you in the garden; I was afraid because I was naked, so I hid." (Gn. 3:10)

And with that admission of fear, it begins! Fear of Pharaoh and his oppression of his Israelite slaves led to *the* "sacrament" for all of Judaism: Moses and the exodus from Egypt. This event represents the outward sign, after all, of God's yearning to free us from bondage and all the fears that slavery, by its very nature, generates. And in the wilderness, when the Israelites lost heart, God spoke thus:

> Do not take fright, do not be afraid of them. Yahweh, your God, goes in front of you and will be fighting on your side as you saw him fight for you in Egypt. In the wilderness, too, you saw him: how Yahweh carried you, as a man carries his child, all along the road you traveled on the way to this place. (Dt. 1:29-31)

Assurance after assurance of God's fidelity did not quell the fears from rising. The prophets, therefore, continued the echo:

> Do not be afraid, for I have redeemed you.
> I have called you by your name.
> You are mine. (Is. 43:1)

Again, when all seemed lost, Jeremiah spoke for Yahweh, saying:

> I have heard a cry of panic, of terror, not of peace.
> . . . But (Jacob) will be freed from it.
> . . . So do not be afraid, my servant Jacob
> – it is Yahweh who speaks.
> Israel, do not be alarmed. (Jer. 30:5, 7, 10)

Yahweh God yearned and continues to yearn for us to know who God really is – not a God of vindictiveness and terror but rather a God who shepherds us, wanting more than anything else to give us a place of refuge, a home truly safe and free of fear. The Psalmist said it best in that classic Twenty-Third Psalm:

> Yahweh is my shepherd, I lack nothing.
> In grassy meadows he lets me lie.
>
> By tranquil streams he leads me
> to restore my spirit.
> He guides me in paths of saving justice
> as befits his name.
>
> Even were I to walk in a ravine as dark as death
> I should fear no danger, for you are at my side.
> Your staff and your crook are there to soothe me.
>
> You prepare a table for me
> under the eyes of my enemies;
> you anoint my head with oil;
> my cup brims over.
>
> Kindness and faithful love pursue me
> every day of my life.
> I make my home in the house of Yahweh
> for all time to come.

We can, of course, reference many other Old Testament sayings which repeat the same message, but suffice it to say here that the entire story of God's involvement with us is to liberate us from our fears through a promise of salvation, of freedom.

In the New Testament, this intent is clearly borne out from the very beginning, in the Incarnation itself, where the angel Gabriel's first words after announcing the good news to the young virgin was, "Mary, do not be afraid; you have won God's favour." (Lk. 1:31)

And Zechariah, filled with the Holy Spirit, spoke the prophecy we call the Benedictus, central to which is the reiteration of God's promised rescue of God's people: "This was the oath he swore to our father Abraham that he would grant us, *free from fear*, to be delivered from the hands of our enemies...." (Lk. 1:73-74)

I suggest that believing in salvation from the bondage of sin ought to result in freedom from fear. Slaves are fearful of their oppressive masters and mistresses; not so freed women and men. We believe that in and through Jesus we have been so freed. Hence our lives ought to reflect this liberation in our attitudes toward all that we fear for ourselves and those we love. Jesus himself clarifies this freedom many times throughout his short, public ministry.

After he calms the storm, for instance, he says to his disciples, "Why are you so frightened? How is it that you have no faith?" (Mk. 4:40). The Gospels also point out, "When the disciples saw him walking on the water and were terrified, Jesus called out to them, saying, 'Courage! It is I! Do not be afraid.'" (Mt. 14:28). And when a sick person asked Jesus to heal him or her, the words would often be words of encouragement, replacing the person's fear with an affirmation of the person's faith. "Courage, my daughter, your faith has restored you to health," (Mt. 9:22) Jesus tells the woman with a hemorrhage. Again, upon hearing of Jairus' daughter's death, he tells the servant, "Do not be afraid; only have faith." (Mk. 5:37). So also Jesus concludes his moving exhortation to trust in Providence by saying, "There is no need to be afraid, little flock, for it has pleased your Father to give you the Kingdom." (Lk. 12:32)

Jesus came to replace fear with faith in God. In this book I will offer you some avenues down which you may find some freedom from your fears, no matter how long you may have had them, no matter how entrenched they may have become.

I am a person who, like many others, is in a process of becoming freed from my fears through faith. In this book I share a part of that process with you. Hence, I write for people who may be seeking from their faith a way to freedom.

Each chapter will begin with the psychological underpinnings of a particular fear, then conclude with Jesus' prescription for handling it, as described in one of his powerful stories we call parables.

I have found that there are four principle areas out of which fears are generated. More often than not, one area merges with another, and differentiating the particular area of a given fear can be quite difficult. Hence, I will separate them for clarity's sake and not as a reflection of reality.

Accordingly, I will first deal with the sources of our fears of God, then utilize Jesus' story of the Good Samaritan to show us a way out of them. Guilt and shame will next be dealt with, and I will use the powerful story of the Prodigal Son to show us a way out of these two painful states. I will then deal with our fear of other people, focusing on the sources of prejudice. I offer Jesus' story of the widow and the judge as a challenging lesson for all of us who want to overcome our fears of others. From there I move into the very personal fears of loneliness and suggest Jesus' story of the talents can offer us a way out of them. Finally, I deal with the fears we have of things, such as fear of the future and fear of death. I conclude by describing the significance of the parable of the sheep and the goats, the last judgment, as an antidote to those fears.

I offer some exercises at the end of each chapter that I hope will help you transfer the lessons from your head to your heart. I believe it is essential that we allow our hearts to become involved if we hope for true freedom to emerge. Use the exercises as you see fit; my intent is to share with you a technique, a way of processing this material that I have found helpful.

I wish you peace as we begin our journey. I wish you courage as you and I face up to our dark side and look forward to the vision that will reveal for us the light that passes all understanding.

– Francis Vanderwall

Other works by the Author...

- *Spiritual Direction: An Invitation To Abundant Life*

- *Water in the Wilderness: Paths of Prayer, Springs for Life*

- *Dynamics for Conversion in Post-Vatican II Lay Ministry: Decrees, Dimensions and Model*

- *Paths of Prayer*
  (Video and audio cassette series)

Freedom
FROM FEAR

Chapter I

FEAR OF GOD

*M*any of us grew up in fear. As children we were often warned that engaging in certain behaviors could bring down upon our little heads the wrath of God. And this divine wrath was terrible to behold, worse still to experience. Hence, we had better do as we are told, or else . . .

As young children, usually before age six or seven, threats of divine vengeance lead to images of God that can be terrifying, fashioning for us a monstrous deity watching over our every move, waiting to catch us in the act. And these acts were usually violations of familial taboos and parental expectations.

"God is going to get you" really meant Mom or Dad were going to get you, so behave yourself according to the expectant norms of behavior Mom and Dad have prescribed for you. Corresponding to the threats, of course, is the anticipated rewards for behaving appropriately; and of all the rewards, the one the child desires most is parental approval and love. The child learns that behaving according to the expected norms of behavior earns her or him this love.

A little child growing up in such a milieu develops, at a very early age, a construct of God that can be quite damaging in later life. He or she rarely gets over these early childhood beliefs about God. Consequently many, if not most, religious practices are undertaken to appease such a God and, it is hoped, to earn God's love in return.

God becomes the internalized parent whom the child both fears and loves. Out of this combination of often conflicting emotions – fear, love, fantasies, hopes, anxieties and affections in relating with one's parents – we find the birth of our own particular God image. As children we swallow whole the God image given us by our parents and other such authorities, for at a young age we have not yet developed the ability to assimilate all the data we are fed.

The God image of our childhood is influenced in later years by various other teachings about the "true" God. Unfortunately, as much as the individual may learn later from other respected sources that God is not a demanding monster, the childhood image persists, albeit to a lesser degree, throughout many people's lives. If we look deep into ourselves, no matter how mature or religiously sophisticated we may have become, a fear of God punishing us for societally unapproved-of behavior and rewarding us for "being good" can be found not far below the surface of our consciousness. And so fear establishes itself as a foundational motive for religious practices, and love becomes something that has to be "earned."

Once I listened to a friend who told me of her fears of God's judgment. She was a very caring, gentle human being, a pillar of her church, looked up to by many in her community, active in several civic organizations. No one would suspect that she did most of these laudable activities out of a fear of God's punishment for her past failures and not out of a genuine selflessness. At least, this was the way she put it when she first told me of her very busy life. I asked her to tell me about her childhood.

Her mother was tyrannical, her father sickly and somewhat of a wimp. Her mother abused her verbally as well as physically on a regular basis. She had been made to feel not just unworthy of affection and love but actually not worthy of being born. Her mother once told her, in a fit of rage, that she tried to abort her when she was several months along in her pregnancy. In fact, the only reason she failed was that the hook of the coat hanger just did not fit quite right. The violence of her childhood contrasted with the serene beauty of the great Northwest, where she grew up amidst giant trees, placid lakes and magnificent blue skies. On a particularly beautiful day she remembered trying to take a nap in the afternoon when she was startled awake by her mother striking her across the mouth with a hand brush. She was about five at the time.

The boundaries of her life were being firmly set, cast in the kiln of daily, irrational violence. And those boundaries confined within them a scared little girl, a girl born scared, as she told me, and confirmed in her fears through persistent abuse. In one way or another she had to prove she was worthy of being alive, worthy of a parent's love regardless of what her mother said of her and did to her.

The terrors of her childhood, naturally enough, became the fears of her adolescence and adulthood, and she found herself, time and time again, placing herself in positions where her sense of unworthiness could be re-affirmed. Her fears of God's terrible judgment and the consequent intensity of her religious activities were desperate attempts to appease this fearsome and demanding God image and earn this God's love someday. Of course, given the ingrained messages of her parental rejection, this was no easy task. It was going to take more than a re-fashioning of her God image. It was going to take serious therapy wherein her own innocence and inherent goodness had to be established, and the separation of her God image from the image of both her parents had to take place. For while her mother was the actual abuser, her father abused her, too, simply by allowing the violence to continue and ignoring her cries for help.

Since our initial conversation she courageously entered therapy and simultaneously received spiritual direction and is now well on the way to recovery. The evidence for this recovery is tangible. She resigned from most of her church and civic activities, re-established herself in a profession she had been qualified in for years though never practiced, and feels like a brand new woman, alive and mostly free of the fears of her former life. Of course, all this took more than three years of hard work on her part, but considering the years of fear, the three or so for healing was a remarkably short time. And her God image changed in the process, from the judgmental, demanding parent, to a God much more like the God Jesus revealed to us as "Abba," Father.

While this story may appear unusual to some, I have found that many people I see in spiritual direction have a God image that generates fear in one form or another, resulting in a life of appeasement, a religion of unceasing atonement. Yet the God imaged for us by Jesus was not a God to be terrified of at all. The God Jesus called Abba, meaning Daddy, was one filled with an overwhelming and infinitely patient love, a God who yearned only for the well-being of His daughter or son, a God whose only motive in sending His son, after all, was our freedom to be, to be ourselves, to be saved from servitude to hard taskmasters and cruel mistresses, a God who indeed was more a nurturing, gentle, caring parent than a stern and harsh one.

Hans Kung writes in his book titled *On Being A Christian:*

"God wills nothing but (our) advantage, (our) true greatness and our ultimate dignity. This then is God's will: *(our) well-being."[1]*

'Fear of the Lord'

The frequently misunderstood admonition to have "fear of God" does not mean to be terrified of God, but rather it means developing an attitude filled with awe, joy, love, honor and glory toward God, author of life, and Creator of a marvelously beautiful universe given to us out of an exuberant love and a generous heart.

Fear of God is all about rejoicing in God's gifts to us and has nothing to do with terror, or a cowering, cringing, submission to God's always-demanding will. It calls for an inner disposition that is of gratitude and thanksgiving, an attitude toward life, all of life, that is buoyant and light, positive and full of hope and laughter and confidence.

I once had a dream in which I was alone in a vast building, similar to a great cathedral in Europe. There was nothing in the building, no altar, no pews or chairs, no statues. The far wall was immense, soaring up into the ceiling and beyond. Covering the wall was something resembling a mosaic rich in various colors, except that this mosaic was shimmering, alive in some strange way. I had an overwhelming sense that I was in the presence of God, the Creator and Supreme Being. I felt an incredible sense of awe and unworthiness for being permitted to be there. Then I saw several other walls, all alive with the same mosaic, at the ends of other great halls, and I was truly overwhelmed. I believe I never felt like this before. Upon waking up I had a sense of great, indescribable peace and I knew what true "fear of the Lord" must be like: awesome, peaceful and steeped in transcendent consolation.

It appears that often the problem with our defective God images must be found not in God but within ourselves and in those authority figures that mediate a God image for us. All too often, religious teachings contradict the teachings of Jesus in this regard.

Religion can breed fear and, in fact, functions in many people's lives as a powerful source of ongoing fear. The numerous laws, rules and regulations of a given religious body seek not only to control people's behavior but dictate people's consciences as well. In this way, fear of breaking religious laws attributed to God frequently becomes the prime concern in an individual's life, precluding any encounter with the true God, the God Jesus called, with that wonderfully intimate word, Daddy. When this occurs, and regrettably it occurs frequently enough, religion becomes an obstacle to encountering God, a hindrance rather than a help. This, of course, is bad religion, but all of us, I believe, are infected to some degree or another with this bug of bad religion which reveals itself in religious practices performed out of fear, not awe, and not out of a heart filled with gratitude and joy.

Neurotic religious fear

Fear, in the religious sphere, can frequently become a neurosis, an escape from reality. For instance, some religious-minded people are obsessive-compulsive neurotics when it comes to worship. We must remember that the repressed emotion in all neuroses is fear.

These people are constantly going to church or talking about God. These are people who possess an abnormal anxiety about their unworthiness before God and are hence constantly trying to appease God through frequent acts of worship, prayers and church activities. They cannot *not* go to church or they cannot *not pray*, and if, on a given day, they fail to go to church, or fail to say their prayers, they become exceedingly uncomfortable.

The emotion functioning behind the discomfort, of course, is fear. And it is fear of a punitive God, one who finds them always inadequate, never quite measuring up.

Yet being in God's presence is a gift, quite unearnable and unattainable through our own efforts. This is not to say we cannot *do* things in order to be disposed toward "seeing" God, but that the actual visioning of God is not based on our efforts but totally on God's yearning for us. Prayer helps us become disposed; worshiping in a community enables us to thank and praise

God, but it is *God's love* that allows us to "see" the truth. Fears keep us from hearing of this love in our hearts, and so our prayers and worship often become exercises to ameliorate our fears, not to encounter the Awesome Love that can be transforming and liberating in its intensity.

Once I had a friend who discussed with me his fear of God's anger toward him. He felt that his past life was so wild, so filled with evil deeds, that God could never want to have anything to do with him, let alone love him. This belief compelled him toward very frequent religious practices. He would go to church once or twice a day, seven days a week. He would actually have to drive to one or two different churches on different days in order to find Masses at the times he could make them between his work and home schedules. He would also try to confess once or twice a week, if not more. His whole world, in fact, revolved around his obsession. Now, he was not, by any means, uneducated. He had a college education, held down a fine professional job and was a pleasant enough person to be around – except for his obsession!

My task was to combat the fear behind his religious practices by trying to help him change his image of God – not an easy task after all these years. I started by asking him to take a period of time off daily for solitude. I avoided using the words "prayer" or "meditation" intentionally, not wanting to feed into his obsession. I then pointed out various scripture passages for him to reflect on, both from the Old and the New Testaments, where God urges us not to be afraid.[2] He promised to do so.

I met with him frequently over the next several months, and slowly, very slowly at times, his image of God started to change. When I felt he was ready, I suggested he skip one of his twice-daily trips to church and spend the time reflecting on God's yearning and acceptance and affection for him instead. Surprising me somewhat, he agreed, and little by little, as his confidence in a God of love, and correspondingly, confidence in himself and his own worth, increased, his obsession was reduced.

It occurred through a process in which he first allowed himself to meet a God of forgiveness and acceptance, then a God who forgave not in the abstract but in actuality, and thirdly a

God who was more concerned for his well-being than anything else. It took time, but as his confidence in the image of a forgiving God increased through the authority of the Scripture passages he faithfully reflected on, so did his confidence in himself increase until he eventually got to the point where he only needed to go to church once a day. But even more important was the changing motive behind his reduced frequency of attendance, from a motive of fear to one of gratitude and thanksgiving. He found a God who accepted and affirmed him for the good man that he was, just as he was, with his weaknesses and failures and past sins not ignored but transcended by love.

The story of my obsessive-compulsive friend, of course, is an extreme case, though not all that unusual in its pattern of behavior. I believe most of us suffer from some degree of neurosis when it comes to the area of religion and fear. In fact, religious rules and regulations can actually be sought after by those who lack conviction and do not have the desire or the interest to take their faith seriously. For these, obeying external rules is an easy way out, for then they do not have to think for themselves; others do it for them. The problem with this approach is that obeying external rules does not do God justice, and all too easily breeds a religion of convenience where a person's investment in God's truth is forfeited for the "truth" taught by a given religion, which may or may not be true.

Since God gave us a mind we ought to use it not only to succeed in life but to succeed in our love relationships as well. And the first of these relationships, indeed the only one that is truly eternal, is the one God yearns to have with us. This, of course, takes thought and study and prayer and perhaps spiritual direction and counseling, and represents "work." But it is work well worth the effort if authentic liberation from religiously motivated fear will be the result. For if we believe God is love, then "in love there can be no fear, but fear is driven out by perfect love..." (1 Jn.4:18)

But for us who have allowed fear to become so much a part of our religious lives, how do we get from here to there? How do we move away from our fear-based lives and move into a life of freedom? I believe the answer is found in a re-discovery of who

God really is.

Now, many of us believe we have a pretty good grasp of who God is, and may feel that further investigation may just be a waste of time. But I suggest that if you journey with me in this investigation you may find a brand new way of living free of fear, through discovering a new image of God, as shown to us by Jesus in his astonishing story we call the parable of the Good Samaritan.

A liberating new image of God:
The Good Samaritan

But the man was anxious to justify himself and said to Jesus, "And who is my neighbor?"

In answer, Jesus said:

"A man was once on his way down from Jerusalem to Jericho and fell into the hands of bandits; they stripped him, beat him and then made off, leaving him half dead. Now a priest happened to be traveling down the same road, but when he saw the man, he passed by on the other side. In the same way a Levite who came to the place saw him, and passed by on the other side. But a Samaritan traveler who came on him was moved with compassion when he saw him. He went up to him and bandaged his wounds, pouring oil and wine on them. He then lifted him onto his own mount and took him to an inn and looked after him. Next day, he took out two denarii and handed them to the innkeeper and said, 'Look after him, and on my way back I will make good any extra expense you have.'

"Which of these three, do you think, proved himself a neighbor to the man who fell into the bandits' hands?"

He replied, "The one who showed pity towards him."

Jesus said to him, "Go, and do the same yourself."

(Lk. 10:29-37)

The parable is all about who God is. God is about compassion. And, this divine compassion has a transcendent dimension to it, for it is not just a compassion that identifies with the sufferings of a fallen stranger but one that risks all in order to liberate the stranger from his or her bondage. And the Samaritan who does this, Jesus teaches us, ought to be our image of who God is. God seeks to free us from our bondage. God seeks to free us from fear. And, of course, in Jesus, that is just what God did. Through this parable we can see that in God there is nothing to fear, especially if we feel in any way an outcast, or a stranger, or indeed sense that we are beaten, abandoned by all, left to die on a lonely stretch of life's road.

The parable begins by depicting a traveler journeying from Jerusalem to Jericho. The traveler is given "everyman" status, for Jesus simply refers to him as "a man," a human being, not a member of any "in" group or "out" group. Often we may feel our fears of God have placed us in just such a place, isolated and alone, not any longer a member of any group, even though we may still carry the membership card with us. In the parable, though, membership is not important; all that matters is that the person is a human being.

Now, this man fell among brigands who stripped him, beat him, and made off, leaving him half dead. This was actually the traveler's own fault. Nobody traveled this seventeen-mile stretch of road alone. All through history this descending road through the desert from Jerusalem to Jericho had been dangerous. The fact that the traveler was attacked on this stretch of road then would not have surprised Jesus' listeners.

Often, it seems to me, we find ourselves on a dangerous stretch of road, and it is our own fault. In spite of warnings, we still proceed, fearful and hoping against hope that we will not be harmed. But then, in a flash, we are stripped, beaten, abandoned, and left nearly dead. Our life is "ruined," and there appears to be no hope.

At times like these some of us turn to socially sanctioned sources for help, such as priests and "Levites," counselors and well-meaning care-givers. Often they help, but there are times when the "professional distance" hinders genuine aid. And, as a result, one may feel even more afraid, even more abandoned and misunderstood. This is not anyone's fault necessarily. All of us have been trained and conditioned to behave in a certain way in a given situation, and our belief system, supported by our society, approves of our behavior, as in the case of the priest and Levite.

The priest came from a legalistic religious mindset that had distinct prohibitions concerning helping strangers. Furthermore, the man could have been dead, and contact with a dead body would defile the priest. Kenneth Bailey, author of *Poet & Peasant* and *Through Peasant Eyes*, points out that the priest collects, distributes and eats tithes. If he defiles himself he would not be able to do any of these things and his family would suffer the consequences with him. This priest was therefore in danger of contracting ritual impurity. Now, maintaining ritual purity was considered the best way of avoiding sin and attaining heights of sanctity.[3] So, the priest was therefore simply trying to follow the dictates of his religion. For him, obeying rules and regulations gave him security and provided guarantees for salvation, a black and white world that had simple solutions to all of life's difficulties, up to now. Not surprisingly, he passed by on the other side, again following the law that said he could not approach closer than four cubits to a dead man without being defiled. J.D.M. Derrett, in *Law in the New Testament,* points out that this was really appropriate behavior since the command not to defile was unconditional while the command to love was conditional.[4]

Now, we have a Levite coming to the place, and when he sees him he passes by on the other side. The Levite would most certainly have known there was a priest ahead of him. Bailey explains that a traveler on this road is extremely interested in who else is on the road. His life may depend on it. Jesus' audience would have assumed this as a matter of course. Further, the Levite could have rendered aid to the wounded man since he was bound by less stringent rules than was the priest.[5] In his book, *The Parables of Jesus,* Joachim Jeremias notes that the Levite was only required to observe ritual cleanliness in the course of his cultic activities, so if the Levite was journeying from Jericho to Jerusalem to perform his official duties he still could have cared for the man; he could have touched him although he might have been dead. But he did no such thing and passed by on the other side as well.[6]

A fearful person is one who often feels he or she is a failure. When "official" care-givers don't care for him or her, the inner conviction of being unworthy is re-enforced. This naturally gets translated into a feeling of inadequacy and unworthiness before God, and God is perceived to be uncaring and concerned more about "ritual impurity" and "ritual cleanliness" than about a fearful, half-dead stranger. The tragedy of such a perception is that nothing can be further from the truth. While God's care-givers may at times be more concerned about rules and laws, God is more concerned, indeed much more concerned, about people, especially people who may be wounded and left for half-dead by society. This is now well-illustrated as the parable continues.

Samaritans were very much outcasts, and in fact people who were considered demon-possessed for many despicable acts committed against the Jews. For instance, Jeremias notes, Samaritans, between A.D. 6 and 9, at midnight during a Passover had defiled the Temple court by strewing dead men's bones, hence preventing the celebration of the feast. They were also people of mixed breed, for they had intermarried with pagans and were therefore considered racially impure. Samaritans were not believed capable of doing good.

The Samaritan sees the half-dead stranger and is moved with compassion. The word used in the Greek language for compassion is very strong, *esplanchnizomai*, implying his bowels were turned inside out at the sight.[7] Moved by compassion, the Samaritan proceeds immediately up to the wounded man and cares for him out of his own resources.

In his book titled *The Gospel in Parable*, John Donahue writes:

"Compassion is the bridge between simply looking on injured and half-dead fellow human beings and entering their world with saving care.... The compassion of God stands behind the coming of Jesus. Compassion is that divine quality which, when present in human beings, enables them to share deeply in the suffering of others."[8]

The actions of the Samaritan spell out what the actions of Divine love contain. First, "He went up to him and bandaged his wounds, pouring oil and wine on them." The bandage he would have used was probably his own turban. The Samaritan hence right away puts himself out for the sake of this stranger, for not wearing a turban in a hot, desert climate exposes one to the possibility of sunstroke. But there is also a theological significance, in that binding up his wounds is mentioned first. This order of doing things, of first binding and then pouring the oil and wine, Derrett points out, represents "the imagery used of God as he acts to save the people."[9] God saves, God binds up wounds, and God uses a hated, rejected outcast of society to do so. Furthermore, pouring oil (to clean and soften the wound) and wine (to disinfect it), while reflecting First Century first aid practices, also represented the elements of the daily temple sacrifice. Ironically, the Samaritan then offers the true sacrifice, on the side of the road, that the priest and the Levite were on their way to perform in the temple.

But the sacrifice continues. The Samaritan now puts the man on his own mount and leads it to the inn and takes care of him. He acts as servant. In the Middle East, who rides and who walks is an important distinction. Servants walk; those of higher rank ride. This Samaritan becomes servant for the sake of a stranger. Furthermore, he not only takes him to the inn but takes care of him there. Bailey points out that there were no inns in the middle of the desert; he would have taken him to Jericho.

Now, the custom of blood revenge in the Middle East meant that the Samaritan could have been killed by the wounded man's family or extended family in retaliation for the man's wounds. The custom was that if the actual assailant could not be found then anyone related to him in the remotest way may suffer instead. The Samaritan was hence taking a very serious personal risk by caring for this wounded stranger overnight.

But not only that, the next day he pays two denarii to the manager of the inn and says, "Look after him, and on my way back I will make good any extra expense you have." The Samaritan has not only compensated for the failures of the priest and Levite but now even compensates for the robbers, Bailey notes.[10]

But there is a further point that I believe is crucial for understanding who God really is. Innkeepers of First Century Palestine were an unsavory lot. If a guest had no money to pay for his or her stay, he or she would have the guest arrested till they did. The wounded man had no money, obviously, and if the Samaritan had not paid for him in advance he would have been imprisoned.

This reveals the decisive dimension of Divine Love: It must be a compassion that liberates. In this, Jesus reveals the kind of love God offers us, a love that not only does one never have to fear, but a love that liberates us to become well again. And this love is extended to all people, not just a select few.

In the early centuries of Christianity, Jesus was seen as the Good Samaritan, and as God's Son he is the classic depiction of the nature of the true God. This God, our God, is like a Samaritan who cares for us when we are abandoned and fearing for our lives.

How God liberates us from our fears

But, we may ask, how does God liberate us from our fears? Those of us who may still have an image of God as magician may expect God to wave a wand and so liberate us. But Jesus contradicts such a notion and instead presents us with a totally different and somewhat shocking image. By depicting himself as the Samaritan, what Jesus is saying is that God can save even through outcasts of society, those, in other words, who can identify with our fearful state because he or she has been there already. And it is by sharing our fears and entering into them that God achieves freedom for us. For if we believe that our God is fearing with us in our fears then we know we are not alone in them. This awareness, of itself, liberates us from within, for a shared fear liberates while a fear experienced alone paralyzes.

God, if we allow God's presence to be felt in our lives, empowers us from within, therefore, and encourages us to use all the resources we have to become free from our fears and so assume our rightful place as dearly beloved daughters and sons of God.

What are these resources that will help to free us? I suggest two key resources. First, choosing a time for solitude daily. I avoid the word prayer because for many, unfortunately, prayer is associated with an activity we do, while solitude represents a state in which God can act in us. We merely set the stage by making ourselves available to God by stilling our minds and so

opening ourselves to the actions of God. The second key re-
source is talking to someone about our fears. Sharing them with
a spiritual director or counselor can be a marvelous act of liberation in itself.

Conclusion and Summary

In this chapter I have tried to share some reflections on how
to move away from being terrified of God to a place where God
is seen not only as benevolent but anxious to befriend us and
become our way to freedom from fear. I did this by using the
parable of the Good Samaritan to illustrate that, in Jesus' understanding, God is not only our way out of a fear-based life but
indeed is the way to a brand new vision of reality in which freedom becomes a genuine interior disposition for us and not merely
an unfulfilled hope. I suggested that a way to realize this new
vision was through seeking solitude and receiving spiritual direction or counseling. Before I conclude this chapter, however,
I want to offer you some exercises that may help you use your
time of solitude to greater advantage.

Prayer Exercise

1. Begin by choosing a time during which you will not be distracted. Set aside about 30 minutes initially.

2. Become still, close your eyes if you wish and take a few deep breaths. I find it helpful to recite the name of Jesus as I breathe in, and recite a named fear or anxiety as I breathe out.

3. Let yourself feel your wounded state. Then sense Jesus, as the Good Samaritan, gazing upon you with great love and compassion in His eyes. He touches you gently. Let yourself feel the power of his touch, warm, gentle, yet firm, flowing through your body, bringing an inner glow. Stay here for a few minutes, savoring the feeling.

4. You hear Jesus say to you, a word like *peace, love, healing, freedom.* You repeat it to yourself, pausing each time to really feel the power of your prayer word taking hold within you.

5. If you find yourself getting distracted just repeat the prayer word, or repeat the name of Jesus.

6. You may wish to conclude your prayer here, or go on to any one of the following exercises.

Use these same steps to help you enter into the other exercises you will find at the end of each of the chapters throughout this book.

The Fear Inventory
(An Exercise)

You may find it useful to answer the following questions and complete the sentences. There are no right or wrong answers; only *your* answers.

1) When I was a little child I feared (specify the person) the most because:

2) After him/her, I feared (specify the person) because:

3) I gradually succeeded/failed in overcoming these fears as a result of:

4) In childhood I imaged God as:

5) As I grew up, God became for me a (specify image):

6) Now, as an adult, to me God is a (specify image):

7) Religion in my childhood consisted of the following activities:

8) As I grew older I regarded religion as:

9) Now, as an adult, I regard religion as:

10) Did fear of failing to perform certain religious obligations preclude me from God's love? What were these obligations?

11) Do I still feel this way? If so, why? If not, why not?

12) Do I genuinely wish to acknowledge my religiously motivated fears and do I genuinely wish to take practical steps to transcend them? What does that mean for me? If so, why? Why not?

Fear
(A poem for meditation)

What violent snag has entered
my heart, ripped through the tender
muscles of my life's central station
and held me captive?

Why have I let myself be imprisoned?
Once at the table of our Lord, I heard
a sudden voice. "Why are you afraid
of Me," it whispered.

An ocean of mercy washed over me
in that moment. My little answers
did not matter, so much riffraff
they were in that immense body
of God's saving waters.
Once, years later, I heard someone else recall
a similar experience. "I heard God
whisper," she said, "why are you afraid?
There is nothing to fear."

And yet I have been lost again
and again, my friends floating
on their own lifeboats in the torn
ocean surface beneath the hurricaned
skies. Why do our enemies
misunderstand, we have cried,
never wanting to be misunderstood,
yet we battle on these life rafts,
each of us trying to survive the storms
of our own lives. How easy to
misunderstand, to fear those
we think our enemy.
We are all
on the same
ocean.

(Continued)

How then so unlike God I have been,
so foolish in my fear of One
who means no harm, of One
who waits on the shore for the
floodwaters to recede, the One who
parts the clouds and makes the sun
shine, who reforms the wet earth
again, and makes grain grow
and fills the air with the music
of the wind.

How could I not hear and answer
when the One who loves me whispers,
"Why are you afraid, my Beloved?"

◆

The Good Samaritan
(A poem for meditation)

Today I learned of a friend's death.
He had been dying for more than a year,
yet it happened that he died on a
day that I was leaving town and, in fact,
had left before the news of his death
was known. So when I returned from a
trip, I learned that he had died and was
already buried.

I cry for him tonight and for myself
who missed his last moments on the road.

He was the Good Samaritan, not I.

He is the one who found me on the road
of his journey, the one who told us of his
dying, who shared in honesty his fear
of being left like one abandoned –
as he was, alone in a hospital room.

I remember the meals he enjoyed,
the stories he told. He has left us
with a startled silence.

Compassion, says our God, is what I
ask of you. If you would be forgiven
and loved, you must first forgive each other –
and even before that you must forgive
yourselves your failures.

Then you can know love.

Then you will be able to let me
forgive and love you whenever
I find you along the road,
dying and stripped of every
garment that you thought
defined you.

An Exercise for the Good Samaritan

Become aware of Jesus' presence in your midst. It is not necessary to detail what He looks like, just sense His presence.

Jesus speaks to you, saying, "I am very pleased with you, and your desire to do the right things in your life for the sake of my kingdom."

How do you feel when you hear these words from Jesus? Stay with those feelings for awhile.

Jesus then says, "Do you wish to go beyond your expectations?"

Do you? Even if you fear going beyond them, try to do so now, in faith. Tell Jesus you would like to, with His help.

Jesus promises to help you. Do you trust His promise of help?

He asks you to think of one person less fortunate than you at this moment in your life. Who is that person?

Take your time feeling compassion for that person in your deepest self. You may need extra time if you find that person instinctually offensive to you.

What does Jesus say to you next?

Stay with his words and the feelings they may generate within you until you feel at peace within yourself.

Chapter II

GUILT AND SHAME

*F*ear manifests itself in many ways throughout our lives. Two particularly common ways are found in guilt and shame. Most of us have felt guilty and all of us have felt the blood rush to our faces in shame at some time or other in our past. While guilt and shame originate from two related though different places, we usually feel the same embarrassment over them and don't pause to ask whether it is guilt or shame that we are feeling.

Sources of guilt

Guilt and the feelings it produces come from a conflict within us over some action taken or not taken that violates the internal sense of right or wrong that we have developed in our lives. Hence, guilt is fundamentally a violation of our internal authority, or conscience.

Unhealthy guilt generates a particular form of anxiety and hence is a form of fear – a fear of being found out, caught and punished. If not found out, guilt inflicts punishment regardless and can actually be worse than the punishment society or an external authority figure would mete out for the offense. So, guilt is an internal judge, jury and executioner. Guilt is something one takes upon oneself and in fact is instinctual in the sensitive person of mature conscience. He or she knows right away that the action is wrong.

In his book, *Guilt: Theory and Therapy*, Edward Stein defines guilt as a state of tension or anxiety over internalized aggression (self-hatred) or loss of self-love. It is the result of the violation of some internalized value rooted in an emotional relationship. It is an after-the-fact punitive system.[1]

Guilt presumes freedom to do something evil against one's internal authority, that voice of conscience within us which, we are taught, is the voice of God. True guilt, therefore, consists of choosing freely to break with a significant love relationship that, by definition, ought to be primarily a relationship of love and not of fear.

How many are aware enough, let alone free enough, to deliberately choose to break a love relationship of this kind, is anyone's guess. My experience has been that most – I would conservatively estimate about 60 percent of professed Christians – do not have a give-and-take mature love relationship with God and are hence not even conscious that their feelings of guilt ought to be connected to the fracturing of a love relationship. The consequence of this unawareness is that true remorse or sorrow for the wrong committed is rare. Usually what I have found in myself is not really sorrow at all but a preoccupation with the self, a wounded pride that shakes the head in disbelief, lamenting, "How could I do that deed" instead of "How could I betray my love."

True guilt has little to do with fear of punishment, but has to do with sorrow for fracturing a relationship of trust, compassion, and unconditional acceptance. It is, however, precisely because of the presumption that these characteristics existed in the relationship prior to the fracture that true sorrow after the fracture can lead not to despair but to hope.

For, since the love was previously strong, it can be safely presumed that knowledge of the true God was strong and this knowledge would lead the individual to seek a reconciliation as soon as possible with the God of his or her heart, confident that indeed the reconciliation will occur. For the guilty one will know that God is love in a very existential way already, and knowing that, such a person will have no fear of seeking reconciliation.

The fear inherent in neurotic, unhealthy guilt depends on the level of self-loathing present. Such a method of recovering "love" depends on the moral development of one's conscience, and conscience in turn is dependant on one's moral formation and understanding of God. Furthermore, neurotic guilt never works in the long run, for the fractured "love relationship" is not true love. Edward Stein notes that neurotic guilt is narcissistic and concerned more about the punishment than reconciliation with the other.[2]

The source of our conscience initially depends, of course, on those lessons taught us from our infancy which we absorbed into our very being. As we grew up, these lessons, learned from our parents, were multiplied through exposure to other authority figures in our lives – teachers, religious authorities, older sisters and brothers, the police, and so on. Eventually we developed a fairly good idea of what was socially approved and acceptable and what was not. Hence, we developed a conscience to hang our moral hats on, as it were.

The content of our conscience now depended on our primary authority figures, and whether there was a relatively stable environment in which we had space to develop. Unfortunately, in contemporary society stable childhood environments are becoming increasingly rare, and consequently fewer and fewer children have the opportunity to form a conscience for themselves that will be acutely tuned toward the well-being both of the child himself or herself and the society in which the future adult will live.

Sources of shame

Guilt presumes at least a developing conscience, a sense of an internal authority, ideally one of love, whose norms have been violated. Shame, on the other hand, fears being caught by the significant others in society.

Tom Hart, a well-known writer in spirituality, told me of a nice description a boy got in a confirmation class: Guilt tells me I made a mistake; shame tells me I am a mistake. Insofar as shame is an interior feeling, it, too, can cause great pain and discomfort similar to guilt. But shame has to do with embarrassment for violating external norms and not necessarily internal ones.

Shame develops before guilt and functions out of the messages of infancy – 15 months to three years, according to Erik Erikson's stages of psychosocial development. It is during this period that negative feelings of worthlessness are established. These feelings say, "I am no good; I am a scum; I will never make it in life," and the person actually believes that these sayings about oneself are true.

Guilt, on the other hand, presumes an internal authority, or conscience, and develops between ages 3 and 6, according to Erikson. In certain segments of society today, for various economic, cultural and social reasons, individuals do not even reach that "guilt stage." A shame-based society is the result.

In the preface of one of his penetrating books, *Healing the Shame that Binds You,* John Bradshaw differentiates between healthy shame which reminds us we are human, and toxic shame in which we believe that we are defective as human beings. It becomes our identity. Toxic shame compels us to lie about ourselves, creating a false self to cover up the flawed and defective self. Toxic shame becomes the source of our neuroses, violence, and criminal behavior. It binds us in a lie about ourselves, and we act out of that lie.[3]

We read daily of children who have already become criminals, of schools that are more like armed camps, and ghetto housing that all too frequently is but a cover for drug dealing and the violence that accompanies it. We also hear of the middle and upper classes of society engaging in deviant social behaviors ranging from so-called white-collar crime to junk bond frauds that harm others with impunity and often result in minimal correction. The rapidly changing geo-political milieu of our day inflicts extraordinary hardship on families through civil wars and revolutions, and society as we knew it often seems to be a thing of the past.

Once I read about a 12-year-old boy living in a single-parent home who shot and killed a fellow student at school. They had been playing minutes before the shooting and then the murdered student, disliking a move the other child had made in the game they were playing, taunted him about his mother and her nightly activities, inferring that her behavior was causing him to cheat in the game. The 12-year-old boy stopped in his tracks at the taunt and screamed at his companion to take back what he said. He not only refused but added insult to injury by pointing out that he did not even know who his father was.

The 12-year-old rushed his companion and they got into a fight. The taunter, being bigger than the 12-year-old, was winning, when, suddenly the smaller boy pulled a gun and shot his companion at point blank range in the face. The boy died on the way to the hospital. Incidents such as this, with perhaps lesser intensity and some variations, take place almost daily in our elementary schools. Children are killing children.

To speak of a well-formed conscience based on a God of love in the face of these realities would then appear ludicrous. Yet, I believe it very necessary that we do so.

When the folkways of a people change rapidly it is clear that the people themselves are changing. Some structures that once sustained a relatively stable lifestyle no longer have relevance, let alone significance. In the face of these foundational changes of societal structures, I believe it is most important that we re-capture the essence of what it means to be human, and re-write the script of our own lives, as it were, based on this re-discovery. And central to this process, I suggest, ought to be a re-capturing of the essentials of a good conscience. This implies understanding the meaning of goodness itself.

Essentials for a 'good conscience'

Fundamental to a "good conscience," I believe, is a respect for one's self, and so for one's neighbor. This means that an environment that fosters self-respect must be developed. If a child is abused on a regular basis, either verbally, physically or sexually, adults aware of the abuse must not ignore it, or make excuses for it, or hope it will go away. They must act to ensure the child is removed from that environment immediately and placed in a safe, nurturing emotional space.

Respect for self and others, of course, applies to all aspects of one's life. This implies caring for one's physical health, as well as one's mental and spiritual well-being. I feel this is an appropriate way of responding to God's astonishing revelation: that we are nothing less than God's own daughters and sons. But respecting ourselves, albeit the essential first step, ought to flow out naturally into a respect of our neighbor. It is not possible, after all, to give what we do not have; hence, self-respect and self-esteem are prerequisites for a respect of neighbor.

But how many of us really have an adequate self-esteem? So much of how we view ourselves, after all, is based on how we see others viewing us. And this perception, which I think more often than not is inaccurate, determines how we feel about ourselves. If we feel we are fat, or plain, or reserved or brazen, then we allow this perception to govern our behavior. When we allow this to happen, no matter if everyone around us tells us it is not true, we feel bad or inadequate and allow that negative feeling to govern our relationships.

If we want to develop an adequate self-esteem it is essential, I believe, for us to hear, from deep within ourselves, the little voice of truth speaking to us. This voice, if we allow it to speak – and this happens mostly when we are in solitude – will assure us that we can be good and beautiful and kind and lovable, that we can be precious to others, especially significant others, and that we are, in fact, immensely valuable and loved by God.

But to hear this voice requires not only an open heart but also an understanding of why we do not have the self-esteem we would like to have. The answer for this lies in our childhood, in those "tapes" we listen to over and over again that were first inserted into our little minds from the very beginning of our days on this earth.

Once a friend of mine was going through a stage of great fear in her life. She told me that it grew so bad she could not even get out of bed in the morning. It had all been triggered by her sister's anguish. Her sister had been receiving "letters of rage" from their mother in which her mother reiterated in harsh and downright unkind words what she thought of her daughter. Evidently her daughter was seen as a failure in her mother's eyes, no good, ungrateful, unworthy of a mother's love. Obviously these letters tore at her sister's heart. When she shared the letters with my friend, my friend became aware that what these letters were saying of her sister certainly applied to her as well. Her mother had said so to her over the years, although each time couched in terms of concern and love for her well-being. As she read the letters, it sank in very deeply that the self-esteem she lacked throughout her adult years really came out of a fear that her mother didn't think much of her as well. That realization threw her into a deep depression that actually immobilized her.

While lying in bed, often with helpless and fearful tears streaming down her face, she came to another realization. The tapes of her childhood came from a mother who was not at all a very motherly person.

"I also saw," she said, "that I would never have the mother I wanted, not in this life, at any rate." At this point, her tears turned into deep sobs that went beyond the tears and pierced her heart at its very center. It was then that she became paralyzed with fear. The fear emerged through a process in which desires for retribution for her wasted life, guilt for feeling such anger toward her own mother, and a sense of hopelessness, all rolled into one, left her in a state of paralysis. She realized her adult life was all about suppressing her true self and living out the tapes of her childhood in order to prove her mother's judgment of her right.

This state of paralysis went on for about three months. During this time she tried to pray but to no avail. Her nearly complete lack of self-esteem, coupled with her anger, made prayer almost impossible.

One day a very good friend visited her from another city. She shared with her what had been going on in her life. Her friend was most empathetic and caring. Then she got a bright idea. (We can call it a graceful insight.) She asked her friend whether she would do some role-playing with her. The friend readily agreed.

"I want you to sit in that tall-backed chair over there," she pointed out, "and become my mother. Then I am going to tell my mother everything I have always wanted to say to her but never could."

This they did. Even now she recalls how astonished she was at how the words just poured out of her. She told her mother how fearful she had made her, how guilt and shame had thoroughly permeated her life, making her feel like the worst person on earth.

"Because of the negative messages you gave me I never felt I could accomplish anything in life. I suppressed my talents, I let others tell me what to do, and allowed my own uniqueness to become squelched and hence silenced. My life has been governed by fears as a result, and for this I am very angry with you," she continued.

The session proved most cathartic, though not without great pain. She started vomiting violently over and over again during the three hours or so that the session lasted. Finally, she exhausted herself and lay down limp and drained.

The experience turned out to be a watershed experience in her life. It started what she describes as her second journey.

"I faced the truth," she said, "and from that time on I started to heal."

She is now active in pursuing her dream, quite involved in several charitable organizations, and for the first time feels she is asserting herself in her marriage and accordingly becoming true to herself and her talents. She receives ongoing spiritual direction and feels that for the first time in her life she has a meaning and a purpose independent of what others say it ought to be.

Sources of low self-esteem

What is the main source of our low self-esteem and feelings of inadequacy? I believe it is fear. Fear functions in much of our behavior because being approved of by others, especially significant others, is foundational to our sense of well-being.

Measuring up to others' expectations as a way of life, however, can cripple us, prevent us from ever really maturing, and consequently can be a prime inhibiter of an authentic, unique individual emerging. Further, we will never measure up to the expectations of others, and in fact ought not to, unless we wish to remain in perpetual adolescence.

Then why do we worry so much about pleasing other people, especially those who claim some authority over us? Because of our childhood upbringing and subsequent training that informed us that not doing so makes us a bad boy or bad girl. We fear the clicking tongues of disapproval and prefer to be untrue to the unique self God has called us to be rather than run the risk of being called "bad" by society's guardians.

We fear the shame; we fear the guilt. Why? Because we fear that "they" – first people, then God – will reject us. "They," when we were infants, were crucial to our well-being. If we behaved contrary to their norms, they might withdraw their love.

Many of us, mostly unaware of our true motivation, are really responding to the important people who enter our lives as if they were our parents and we were infants desperately in need of their approval for survival.

Further, society and religion have imposed their own sets of rules, regulations, laws and precepts upon our heads. Most of these were imposed on us when we were young, albeit after our parental authorities did so. So fear, manifested in shame or guilt, becomes fear not only of losing parental love but fear of being condemned to hell or excommunicated from the church, or, at very least, publicly or privately sanctioned. Following the rules as prescribed to us by parental, church or societal governing bodies assures us that we are good, approved of and accepted.

Feelings of guilt result from violating norms that we have internalized without masticating them, i.e. without chewing on them, like a cow chewing her cud, and without spitting out that which does not feel right and swallowing that which does. If we lead our lives trying to conform to unmasticated rules belonging not to ourselves but to someone else, guilt can become our frequent companion. On the other hand, if we function out of internalized shame, a sense of hopelessness will pervade all that we do. And what we do will be mostly maladaptive – overwork, manipulating others, perfectionism, repression of feelings, projections and denial.

"Fitting in," being an accommodating individual, a conformist, is actually prized by all governing bodies, from prison guards to people in big business and church leaders, and in reality is a desired goal of living for many. Unfortunately, realizing this goal guarantees that one will have difficulty becoming a unique individual. It will also not permit any personal dreams, hopes and longings to become fulfilled.

We can spend so much time, consciously or otherwise, trying to please others that we cease being true to ourselves. Then, Shakespeare's challenge, "to thine own self be true," remains a meaningless thing, whistling in the winds.

We can betray ourselves, who we are, who we hope to be, and who God longs for us to be someday, in warding off the unpleasantness of guilt or shame. The solution is to stand on our own two feet, think for ourselves, integrate that which is good from external authorities into our internal system of right and wrong, and then live by that internalized system.

Doing this takes enormous courage and hard work. It demands that we grow up, take risks, and learn from failures rather than allow failures to be the catalysts that excuse us back into our conformist, untrue and false selves. If this happens we will be left with this lament: "Once I tried to be true to myself but I got shot down so now I am living out my life in a fearful state of compromise and half-lies." Of course, we will not really say this to ourselves, but at times we may feel it, in a sadness that seems to come from nowhere.

The challenge for all of us who believe in a God of unconditional love is two-fold: First, to make a choice to take steps necessary to become a unique individual, free of inordinate fears; and, secondly, to manifest our belief that God is truly a God *for* us, and not against us, by boldly daring to live out our dreams, hopes and longings.

James Fowler, in his classic study of the stages of faith development in a person's life, notes that for many adults a synthetic-conventional faith (Stage 3 of 6 stages) works well because it provides a permanent place of equilibrium. This stage forms in adolescence, when a person's religious yearning is for a God who knows, accepts and confirms the self deeply, and provides the self with an infinite guarantee of self-worth. Authority from without becomes the authority within and what "they" think matters more than what "you" think. And when "they" speak for God, "you" dare not question them for fear of losing self-worth in the eyes of God. This is why religious institutions "work best" if most of its members belong to Stage 3. It is a conformist stage in which one's faith has synthesized values and information from adolescence and receives ongoing affirmation from the society around the member.[4]

Once I was told of a man in his forties who had only recently admitted to himself that he was gay. He was in extraordinary pain over it, convinced that God had condemned him to eternal hellfire already and that he had no hope of ever escaping his fate. All the teachings of his church, all that he had learned from his parents and religion teachers in school, confirmed his worst fears. He had consulted a priest and had gone to confession, he said, but the priest only reiterated what he already believed, and he felt worse than before.

In this state he visited a colleague of mine. She listened carefully to his anguished account, and then asked him whether he really believed God had already condemned him. He looked at her and said nothing for a long time. Then he spoke:

"I feel in my head that that is what the God I was taught to believe in would do, but I also feel in my heart, that is not true. I feel there is a God, the One who made me, who accepts me, and may even love me."

She urged him to listen to his heart then and begin to redefine his God-concept from a more adult, and educated, point of view. She assured him that not only had God not condemned him, God was anguishing with him. Again, he listened to her and said nothing for long time. Finally he nodded in agreement.

"I must believe that," he said, "for as you spoke I felt within me a small sense of hope."

She went on:

"Remember that Jesus befriended tax-collectors, prostitutes and sinners, outcasts of his society, offering them a forgiveness and a hope that their religion would not give them."

"Yes," he said, "but Jesus befriended them so that they would change!"

"True," she said, "but many of them could not change; they were stuck in what they were doing."

She recalled for him the prayer of the tax-collector, "God, be merciful to me, a sinner" (Lk. 18:14), and what Jesus said of him, that he went home justified, though the Pharisee did not. He listened to her words very carefully and then after another long, now characteristic, pause, he smiled.

"Thank you," he said. He left with a sense of peace and acceptance he had not felt in years.

His God-concept had begun to be redefined, and he had glimpsed, however briefly, a God who would be with him in his future struggles and not against him. He left with some hope for the future. I believe he experienced, albeit briefly, the grace of the Sacrament of Reconciliation.

Guilt and shame, while originating in different places in our developing psyche, both have fear as a fundamental underlying emotion. With guilt, it is a fear of violating the norms of one's conscience, that entity many Christians believe is the voice of God dwelling within the individual. If God is seen as ultimate love then the fear in guilt ought to be found in offending this love. Guilt can also be seen as denigrating or betraying one's own self-love, one's own self-worth. Shame is similar in that the fear it comes out of is fear of violating the norms of other people, especially significant others, in one's life.

Prescription for dealing with guilt and shame

In Jesus' teachings we have a remarkable appreciation of what it takes to alleviate our guilt and our shame. He saw – as do some contemporary therapists and counselors, priests and ministers – that the basis and origin of authentic healing of our conflicted selves is found in acceptance.

Edward Stein observes that acceptance is the affirmation to another that unqualified love is given in spite of guilt. The result is that there is hope of a human relationship and even of self-acceptance, so that now the individual can face his or her guilt in all its rawness and seek to do something about it.[5]   Acceptance of the other, with all his or her guilt and shame, was one of Jesus' extraordinary talents. In this He called forth love from the suffering sister or brother, and true reconciliation was the result.

Let us reach back briefly here and try to situate Jesus' amazing acceptance of sinners in the context of His life's mission. In so doing, I hope, we can find a way of healing for ourselves, a way that can free us from the fears of God that we may have in our lives. Let us begin by recalling Jesus' words:

> The Kingdom of God is close at hand. Repent, and believe
> in the Good News. (Mk.1:15)

Jesus came out of the wilderness, where he had fasted forty days and forty nights, and where he had been tempted by Satan to give up his mission. This mission was one of proclaiming a Gospel of repentance in faith wherein hope for the hopeless was announced. This Good News which we call gospel was about a truly revolutionary and radically new way of living, a new way of looking at ourselves, our neighbor and reality itself that would be something brand new on the face of this earth. Jesus termed this "The Kingdom of God."

The central symbol of the Kingdom Jesus proclaimed was of a festive table where the finest foods and the best wines would be served, where there was music and dancing, and where those who in this world were considered outcasts would not only be guests but guests of honor. At this table, accordingly, there were no requirements and indeed no concern for moral purity, ritual correctness, or holiness. Rather, there was a firm belief that the power of the Host could reach all manner of people with an extraordinary and truly purifying love, which would transform all those open to receiving it.

In turn, this love would eventually fashion an entire community, whose only purpose would be to love one another even as the Host was loving them through issuing the invitation. This love was to be something the likes of which worldly communities could only long for, or talk about, for it was a love that was completely and totally without any conditions attached. It was a love in which the invitee would feel so confounded by the host's acceptance that all reprehensible behavior within her or him would melt away. In its place a deeply heartfelt gratitude would appear that would generate a yearning to respond with the same unconditional love and acceptance of his or her neighbor. Love, it was hoped, would then become the contagion that would transform this world.

Jesus sometimes dined with tax-collectors, sinners and prostitutes. These represented morally reprehensible people who engaged in dishonorable professions in order to survive. They certainly carried much guilt and tons of shame with them wherever they went. Tax-collectors were likened to robbers, treated with contempt, for not only did they work for pagan Rome, they extorted extra money from their own people. Sinners were that class of people seen as criminals who did not observe the Torah, or who could not, having disreputable jobs – swine herders, fruit-sellers, bartenders, seamen, pimps, servants. They were deemed "polluting" or "unclean" by religious people. They were badly paid and often abused as a result. Prostitutes were impover-ished, unskilled women. Found mostly in cities, they often lived in brothels. Prostitutes usually were slaves, daughters who had been sold or rented out by their parents, wives who were rented out by their husbands, poor women, the divorced and widowed, single mothers, captives of war or piracy, women bought for soldiers, and women who could not work in middle- or upper-class professions.

By not only dining with but hosting these, Jesus was saying these were the ones who brought blessings on God's house, not the religiously pure. So, when we feel guilty and excluded, re-jected and shamed by society or church or economy, the King-dom of Jesus Christ reaches out to us especially, assuring us that God has cast God's own lot with us and given us the dignity of a daughter or son of God, worthy of sitting at God's own table. A complete acceptance of the outcast is intended; it reflects the true nature of God and God's Kingdom.

This vision of a community of love was the central motif of Jesus' gospel proclamations. It represented a desire on God's part for a heaven on earth, a hope for which the Divine Son, Jesus, put his life on the line. For this kind of a vision – where those of the lower classes and those of foreign smell would all sit down together as one – made no sense at all. It contradicted the wisdom of human tradition far too much for it to be tenable. This Divine dream was so unrealistic and impractical, indeed scandalous, that the guardians of religious orthodoxy hardened their hearts against the messenger and had Him crucified as a warning to anyone else who may have such a crazy notion. The first shall be last, indeed!

Jesus condemned mostly one sin, the sin of obduracy, or hard-ening one's heart against his message, against the Good News of the Banquet and its indiscriminate invitations to all. This sin was refusing to believe in the Good News by trusting more in the power of religion, especially religious laws, to save, and not trust-ing in God's power, which saved through overwhelming acceptance and unconditional love.

Jesus condemned a religion that in the name of God oppressed the disenfranchised, the poor, the helpless, the widow, the tax-collector, the scoundrel, sinners and children. Jesus condemned religious leaders who crippled the outcast, the morally impure, the guilt-ridden, and the rejects of society, by burdening them with impossible requirements as conditions of re-entry into the community.

And, of course, Jesus infuriated just about everyone, at some time or another in His very brief three years or so of public ministry, so much so that his mother and cousins came to take charge of him once, figuring him to be mad. His disciples, who were his closest companions, missed the whole point, hoping, right up to the very end of his days on this earth, right before the Ascension, that the Kingdom he proclaimed would indeed be very much *of* this earth, of power and prestige and rank and position and honor. He not only frustrated their very worldly hope, He ascended into the heavens before their very eyes, and they had to wait in fear and trembling for the Holy Spirit before they understood what Jesus and the Kingdom of God was really all about, though not all of them understood even then.

The teachings of Jesus were all about reconciliation of the repentant sinner with a God of infinite mercy and compassion. There does not seem to be any sin Jesus would not readily forgive except the sin described variously as the sin against the Holy Spirit (Mt. 12:32); the deadly sin (1 Jn. 5:16); and the sin of apostasy, or holding Christ in contempt after accepting Him (Heb. 6:4-6). What is this unforgivable sin? Joseph Martos, in his book, *Doors to the Sacred*, writes:

"Christian theologians have speculated about it for close to twenty centuries, but the simplest answer seems to be the most plausible: it was unrepented sin, the sin of turning away from God without asking for forgiveness."[6] In other words, choosing to remain in guilt, out of fear that the sin is too great to be forgiven, or hiding behind shame as an excuse for refusing to go forward in life.

What are those sins we feel guilt about? I believe they can mostly be reduced to three categories: sins related to sex; sins in which anger toward self or others is manifested; and infractions of the law, either religious or secular.

So what works to relieve us of our guilt and our shame? For guilt, authorities tell us, it is forgiveness, whereas for shame it is acceptance. These two movements I suggest, come under the umbrella of reconciliation. Reconciliation presumes a prior relationship, a relationship of unconditional love and acceptance. But if we have not had such an experience in our past – How many of us can say we have? – then it is difficult to really believe that we are truly forgiven and accepted back.

For this, we need a much deeper appreciation of who God is. Developing such a knowledge begins, it seems to me, with encountering God in a brand new way. Perhaps it was because Jesus knew this that he gave us that most profound parable of the Prodigal Son. The lessons of the parable alone ought to completely change our perceptions of who God really is, and accordingly make it possible to respond with an open heart and mind to the forgiveness and acceptance the Father of Jesus yearns to give us.

In this parable we have a marvelous challenge offered us. We are invited to re-define our image of God, whatever that image may be, to an image of a God of unconditional love. This cannot happen overnight. It takes prayer, patience, spiritual direction and, above all, a *desire* to become free from fear as represented in our guilt- and shame-based lives.

Who God really is:
The Parable of the Prodigal Son

> A man had two sons. The younger said to his father, "Father, let me have the share of the estate that would come to me." So the father divided the property between them. (Lk. 15: 11-12)

The very opening lines of the parable immerse us into an unprecedented event in Middle Eastern society in which a shocking revelation of the true dimensions of Divine Love is offered. By itself it could completely shatter any conceptions we may have of a God who is in any way eager to punish us or hold a grudge against us.

In Middle Eastern society, Kenneth Bailey tells us, the request of the younger son represented an extraordinary insult toward his father. When does a person usually receive an inheritance? After the death of his or her father. For the younger son to request his share of the inheritance of his father was then an incredible insult. He was, in effect, telling his father that he wished him dead.[7]

The normal response of an Eastern potentate to this request would have been a convulsion of rage. He would have not only refused the boy in no uncertain terms, he would have expelled him from his house immediately with the injunction never to return. Instead, in what must have been a shocking demonstration of impropriety in the minds of Jesus' listeners, this father, without saying a single word, divides the property between his two sons. What he did here had most significant personal implications for the father. It was expected that even if the father had chosen to initiate the division of his "pension" between his two sons while still in good health, the sons had no right to sell the property while he was still alive. The fact that the younger son asked not only for the property but, by inference, the right to sell it, as well, clearly indicates that he did not give any thought at all to his father's welfare. In effect, he cut his father's "pension" in half.

And the father did not say a word. To what was an extraordinary insult, the father humbly, with not even a whisper of protest, gives in to the young man.

What a powerful symbol of Divine Love! Jesus is saying the Father gives in to our unfair demands even though his own "family" will be put into jeopardy as a result; even though his own "future" will be threatened, the Father acquiesces to our demands. Any concept that we may harbor of a God eager to punish us ought to be squelched forever just with this portrait of Divine generosity, let alone with what Jesus is about to relate.

> A few days later, the younger son got together everything he had and left for a distant country, where he squandered his money on a life of debauchery. (Lk. 15:13)

It did not take long for the young son to take advantage of his father's unprecedented action – actually, just a few days. Real estate has to be sold so that it can be translated into cash. This usually takes some time. In this instance, though, it took but a few days. Further, up to this time, the younger son's request and his father's acquiescence to it would have been in-house, a private matter. But, now the younger son goes public. Everyone would know of the foolish action of the father. The father would undoubtedly become the subject of public gossip, and shame would be the result. The father, because of his overwhelming love, has now allowed himself to bear shame, and not a word does he say. And real estate sold in but a few days in all probability would have been sold for less than it was worth. The younger son was eager and he was willing to take a loss to get away from his father and his family.

This must be the finest illustration of what transcendental love means; it demonstrates a God acting foolishly, at least in the eyes of this world, for the sake of an unappreciative son.

Rebellion is usually confronted with harshness by an authoritative force and often crushed ruthlessly and with a sense of satisfaction on the part of the authority, for the right order of things has been restored. And the authority justifies its actions for this reason. Rebellions usually occur in the face of oppression and perceived cruelty. But when the authority is shamelessly benevolent and a rebellion, even a life-threatening rebellion, takes place anyway, what should such a benevolent authority do? It seems the natural worldly response would be for the authority to harden its former benevolence and tighten all restrictions so that the rebellion will not happen again.

But evidently this is not the way of Jesus' Father. He gives in to the rebellious son without a word. Or, maybe, the Father knew something we have yet to learn. If he tried to domesticate his wayward son, he would certainly have maintained law and order but lost his son's potential for loving him in the process, for he would have crushed his spirit and so destroyed his uniqueness. This the father would not do.

I am reminded of the story of the sheep who found a hole in its enclosure and escaped from the fold. The shepherd looked for the sheep for days and found it in the nick of time, for several wolves were chasing it hungrily. The shepherd saved the sheep from the wolves, soothed it, and carried it back safely to its pen.

And in spite of his neighbor's criticisms and ridicule he refused to fix the hole in the enclosure.[8] What a marvelous illustration of liberating love!

And so, the young man converts his share of the estate into money and leaves for a distant country, where he squanders it all on a life of debauchery and prodigal, or extravagant, living.

The young man arrives in a foreign, clearly gentile land, rich and ready to party. He is unknown here, he has no reputation to live up to, he can do as he pleases. And he does.

There is a preoccupation with sexuality in Western religions and consequently debauchery is often connected almost exclusively with sex. But, according to Bailey, the Greek text and the vast majority of the Oriental versions do not condemn the young man for immorality but for being wasteful, for luxurious or indolent living.

I believe this brings up a significant point for a contemporary reading of this verse. The young man takes what is not his and wastes it. Often we, too, tend to take our talents, our education, "the property" God has given us – whatever that may be – and waste it, by not using it well, or not developing it. We allow our fears to compel us into hiding it lest we are found out as undeserving of the gifts we have received – as if gifts or inheritances can ever be deserved! Indolence and luxurious living, what we call conspicuous consumption, is so much a part of our society that we do not even feel the need to justify wasting things, for there is so much material abundance. Furthermore, we argue that we have earned it and have a right to do with our wealth as we please.

But with this God, freedom is granted for us even to waste what we think we earned all on our own with no help from anyone, presumably not even God. God allows us our illusions even though they might lead to our self-destruction. It seems that an aspect of the nature of true love is revealed for us here. Authentic love liberates the beloved even though that liberation involves risk and humiliation both for the liberated as well as the liberator. This is very hard for us to grasp, I think, because we don't love in this way. Our love always has conditions attached to it, and so we ascribe *our* way of loving to God. But God does not love as we do: God loves unconditionally, accepts us as we are, and gives us all the freedom we ask for, even though that may involve our self-destruction.

> When he had spent it all, that country experienced a severe famine, and now he began to feel the pinch, so he hired himself out to one of the local inhabitants who put him on his farm to feed the pigs. And he would willingly have filled his belly with the husks the pigs were eating but no one offered him anything. (Lk. 15:14-15)

We have here a description of utter destitution. The young man had lost not only his entire inheritance but so desperate had he become, he lowered himself to work for a gentile in the most despicable of tasks, indeed for a Jew a task that would earn him exclusion from his religious community.

As we know, pigs, to this day, represent a taboo animal for the Jews. Associating with pigs is bad enough, but actually feeding them would have been unthinkable. Pigs were unclean animals and any Jew associating with them could not observe the Sabbath and would be forced to renounce the regular practice of his religion.[9] Furthermore, his state is so pitiful he is even willing to eat the food the pigs were eating, but no one offered him anything.

The young man had become so much of a non-entity that unclean animals were fed while he could not even get a morsel of their food to satisfy his hunger. He just did not matter to anyone. He could have starved to death for all they cared. In fact, he was doing just that!

Often we, too, have made choices in life that have placed us outside our various groupings – family, religious, economic, cultural and political entities. Often we may feel the sense of isolation and indeed physical and spiritual destitution our actions have put us in, and we may feel shame and guilt over them. We may feel so bad, in fact, that a sense of hopelessness may pervade our days, a depression that won't go away. It is particularly in times like these that we must force ourselves – for it will not come naturally – not to give in to our fears of rejection, but to use our intellects to find a way out of the situation we find ourselves in at the time. Bemoaning our fate betrays an underdeveloped or perhaps erroneous understanding of God and God's yearning to be generous and forgiving of us. But we have to do our part and ask for the help we need.

> Then he came to his senses and said, "How many of my father's paid servants have more food than they want, and here am I dying of hunger! I will leave this place and go to my father and say: 'Father, I have sinned against heaven and against you; I no longer deserve to be called your son; treat me as one of your paid servants.'" So he left the place and went back to his father. (Lk. 15: 17-20)

I have occasionally heard sermons in which the priest or minister made a strong case for the importance of repenting of our sins and returning to God just as the prodigal son did in the parable. The lines he or she quoted were, of course, these verses beginning with the son "coming to his senses." However, scholars by and large do not see this phrase "coming to his senses" as repentance language, though it does contain an element of repentance in it. But the sense of repentance conveyed in the Aramaic has more to do with "changing one's mind" or "reconsidering" rather than the theological concept of repentance usually conveyed by Luke with the word *metanoia*. The fact that Luke does not use technical "conversion" language here makes it questionable about whether this is what Luke intended.

Furthermore, if we reflect on the context, it becomes evident that the young man "came to his senses" only because he was in dire straights. Supposing the country had not experienced a severe famine, and supposing he had not spent his entire fortune on his debaucheries, would he have returned to his father? The evidence of the first part of the story certainly does not allow for such a change of heart.

His planned "confession" further, does not support any sign of a genuine repentance, though he certainly was sorry – for the state he had gotten himself into! He does, however, realize that he had let his father down grievously and had violated some exceedingly sacred moral obligations towards his father. But again, would this realization have been triggered had he not gotten into such sad shape? Probably not.

He was aware, however, that in no way could he hope to be treated as a favored servant. He hoped to be hired as an outsider, a day laborer, uninvolved in the affairs of the estate.[10]

I believe this soliloquy of the younger son depicts quite well the religious sensibility of many of us Christians in our relationships with God. We keep God at a distance, someone we can manipulate when it suits us but not one we seek out as we would an exalted member of our own family when we feel guilty or shameful about some misdeed.

But, regardless, the important action, I believe, is to return even with our less than pure motives perhaps, but, nevertheless, to return – to return home, to the place where inestimable compassion, and forgiveness, and exaltation await us.

Unfortunately, quite often this return home does not take place until we have hit rock bottom, with nowhere else to turn, with no one else to reach out to because no one else is there. But it does not have to be like this. We *can* return before we hit bottom, and we can do so now rather than later.

What must that journey home have been like for the prodigal son? We can but conjecture, of course, from our own experiences. Many conflicting thoughts and emotions must have flowed in and out of that young man's mind. Would his father acknowledge him, would he turn him away without so much as a glance, and would he even get to see his father? After all, his desertion was public knowledge, and his father had probably instructed his many servants to keep him from even coming onto his property. And he knew that since the whole village would have known what he did he certainly would not be welcome there. But the risk had to be taken.

> While he was still a long way off, his father saw him and was moved with pity. He ran to the boy, clasped him in his arms and kissed him tenderly. (Lk. 15: 20)

This verse represents one of the most poignant and consoling passages of the entire Gospel. The father acts. He acts in ways most unacceptable for social propriety of that day and for the rules of reconciliation that should have been followed.

He sees the boy from a long way off and recognizes him. He

must have been looking down the road, perhaps looking down that road many times, yearning for his lost boy's return. It was not his duty to look for strangers down the road; that was his oldest son's job. But this father's heart was so full of longing that he couldn't help himself. He must have looked and looked and perhaps dreamed about one day seeing his younger son returning home.

And now his dreams were coming true. He saw him. Jumping up, ignoring the rules of decorum that would brand him as undignified, he picks up his long flowing robes and runs. Eastern potentates do not run. How they walk reflects on who they are. This father, though, throws all these cautions to the wind, so overwhelmed with love is he at seeing his son, seeing him, no doubt, in a terrible state of deprivation. And so he runs to him.

Bailey notes that this action – so spontaneously one of immense love – also served the purpose of protecting the boy from the hostile villagers. The villagers, upon seeing him, would have shouted insults and perhaps even physically abused him for his actions toward his father and indirectly toward them.

Upon reaching the boy, the father clasps him in his arms and kisses him over and over again in an outpouring of affection, and compassion, and relief at his son's return. The father's warm embrace and public display of such great love represented both forgiveness and complete healing of the relationship so hopelessly fractured by the boy's previous actions. And the son has not said a word yet. There really was no chance to do so, so unexpected and overwhelming was his father's welcome. And it was not necessary.

The "confession" he had prepared was rendered redundant. Yet he had to say it. And so he tries, missing the point in the process. The point, of course, was that the father's actions so transcended the son's calculated request and carefully thought-out proposition that they rendered his entire strategy meaningless.

We have already heard the "confession" in rehearsal, but now in reality we find a major omission, triggered not by the boy but by the father's exuberance over his return. For the text states:

> "Father, I have sinned against heaven and against you. I no
> longer deserve to be called your son." But the father said to his
> servants . . . (Lk. 15: 21a)

The father does not allow the boy to finish his confession. He
breaks in, thus preventing the son from even making the request
to be treated as a paid servant, an outsider. One gets the sense
that in the father's exuberance at his son's return he did not even
hear the first part of his confession. The fact that he was back,
that's all that mattered. But now the father truly becomes the
prodigal, the extravagant one. He goes overboard. He spells
out in shocking ways how very much this return means to him.
For he says to his servants,

> "Quick! Bring out the best robe and put it on him; put a ring
> on his finger and sandals on his feet. Bring the calf we have
> been fattening, and kill it; we are going to have a feast, a
> celebration, because this son of mine was dead and has come
> back to life; he was lost and is found." And they began to
> celebrate. (Lk. 15: 22-24)

The specifications of the father to his servants are explicit and
freighted with meaning. Scholars tell us the best robe that he
ordered the boy adorned with was his own ceremonial robe, worn
on feast days and other great occasions; the ring represents be-
stowal of authority; and the sandals on his feet, a sign that the
younger son was free.[11] Slaves did not wear shoes; only freed
men and women did. The three instructions publicly stated the
son's full reinstatement, and then some. It seems he even receives a higher dignity than he would have had before he left,
with the robe, the ring, and the sandals. But it is by no means
over.

The proper response to such a return must be a great celebration. So the father orders the fatted calf to be slaughtered. This
means that the entire village would be invited. Bailey observes
that if it were going to be only a family celebration, a goat would
have been killed. The great joy of the father is to be shared with
a great many people, indeed the entire community. The father,
in fact, justifies his extravagance, observing that this son of his
was dead and has come back to life, he was lost and is found. It

is almost as if the father is giving his son all the credit for the celebration and not even acknowledging that it was he, not the son, who precipitated the actions that result now in a great celebration. Great love is self-effacing without knowing it, or even caring.

The relationship so grievously and indeed fatally broken is now fully restored. The actions of the father make this possible; the son had only to present himself, even with his calculated motives. It was enough. From then all he had to do was accept his father's overwhelming graciousness. In his book, *The Parables: Their Literary and Existential Dimension*, Dan Otto Via observes that "repentance finally turns out to be the capacity to forego pride and accept graciousness."[12]

The son returned with a legal solution in mind but the love of the father so far transcended his legal mindset as to place him in an entirely new relationship with his father in which all penalties from the law were not only abrogated but not even acknowledged as relevant. Via observes that in the end the prodigal son is free from want and free from law, that is, free from the need to establish his position through his own efforts.[13]

The celebration which concludes this first part of the parable depicts for us a portrait of the heavenly banquet. Often we may wonder what heaven is like. We need to wonder no longer! It is about a celebration of great proportions, where the finest foods and the best wines are served, where there is music and dancing, and where the guest of honor is the least deserving one of all. The Host, of course, makes it all possible. We are but invited to come, just as we are, with all our legalistic and manipulative mindsets, with all our plans and strategies for salvation, and there be confounded by a graciousness that is so overwhelming we can't help being humbled, and repent, and so be liberated to celebrate all of life once again in ways we never even envisioned. All the guilt, all the shame we may have had is transcended by love.

> Now the elder son was out in the fields, and on his way back, as he drew near the house, he could hear music and dancing. Calling one of the servants, he asked what it was all about.

"Your brother has come," replied the servant, "and your father has killed the calf we had fattened because he has got him back safe and sound." He was angry then and refused to go in, and his father came out to plead with him. (Lk. 15: 25-28)

While this astonishing homecoming was taking place, while a banquet was being prepared, while the villagers who were not in the fields had already gathered together at the great landowner's mansion, and had started to celebrate with music and dancing, the elder son was working, assiduously fulfilling his obligations as he always did.

Why did the father not send a servant immediately to summon his elder son from the field upon the arrival of his younger son? Perhaps the father knew his elder son's mentality only too well and figured it was best to leave him out in the fields until the banquet had been prepared, the villagers assembled, the celebration begun. Perhaps the father knew that if he had sent for the older son sooner he would have tried to sabotage the whole process and prevent the banquet from taking place. Certainly, the older son's reaction upon hearing the news proved this later notification justified.

What was the mentality of the older son? I suggest he depicts a mentality reflected in all of us. We all believe, and our society and culture support it, that leading an obedient, hard-working and selfless life earns us certain rights both before God and society. We expect to be looked up to, emulated and treated with the respect we deserve. Concomitantly, we feel justified in looking down on those who do not do the things we do. Unfortunately, this idea of justice breeds a mentality that makes us much like those who we so readily condemn. We feel society owes us; so do many welfare recipients, and so do many out-groups who feel oppressed by unfair labor practices or illicit gains of the powerful. But this we cannot see; our righteousness prevents us from doing so. And so we feel angry, we feel betrayed.

The older brother, because of this mentality, rebelled. He was angry; he had a right to be. He was justified in feeling this way. Fortunately for him, his father did not. If his father had felt this way, if he had a mentality that bred self-righteous indignation, the elder son could actually have been in deadly trouble. According to Deuteronomy 21:18-21, the father or the mother of the stubborn and rebellious son who will not listen to them has a right to order that he be stoned to death by all his fellow citizens at the gate of the town. His father could have had him put to death.

It is very, very difficult for us to grasp how insulting the older son's actions were. The older son violated several cultural taboos upon his return home from work. Bailey observes that "the servant" he called aside was probably not a servant of the master but actually a young boy, a part of the group of young boys participating in the feast going on inside the courtyard, albeit in an unofficial way since only adults attended feasts. This young boy's speech also indicates he was not a servant since no servant would speak of his master as "your father." He would have used far more deferential language. Further, the elder son knew that custom required he act as host, welcoming and caring for guests and certainly showing a special warmth towards his long-lost brother. Any feelings of hostility he may have toward him or his father needed to be buried during the festivities; they could be expressed later in private.[14]

It was certainly a very great public insult to refuse to even go in to a banquet hosted by his father. The break in the relationship with the father caused by this refusal is almost as great as the younger son's, when first he asked for his inheritance. In fact, the penalties for both sons' behavior warranted the ultimate in severity.

But the father, once again most uncharacteristically, comes out to his son. Even as he came out and ran toward his younger son, he now comes out to plead with his older son, speaking to him in a kind and friendly way. This again is unheard-of behavior for an Eastern potentate, especially during a banquet.

> He answered his father, "Look, all these years I have slaved for you and never once disobeyed your orders, yet you never offered me so much as a kid for me to celebrate with my friends. But, for this son of yours, when he comes back after swallowing up your property – he and his women – you kill the calf we had been fattening." (Lk. 15: 29-30)

To a visible demonstration of love, proclaimed publicly, the father receives insult, reproach and condemnation. The elder brother does not even greet his father with a title as he was obliged to do; instead he dives right into his complaints. And his complaints are two-fold: First, that I have slaved for you obediently, and second, that for all I have done, where is my share?

The elder son, just like the younger son, argues from the point of view of a slave: I have *slaved* for you. He misses the point: He is not a slave, he is a son. This so clearly reveals the religious sensibility at work. We feel we have to do things to be found worthy of God's love, and hence fail to see the astounding truth, that we already have received the greatest gift of all, the gift of being God's own daughter or son, with all that that implies. The attitude of slave persists only because, like the elder son, we fail to grasp the overwhelming gift God's graciousness has already bestowed on us – God's entire wealth, God's entire inheritance, God's only Son, God's only Spirit.

Salvation is not about our "slaving;" it is about a transcendent love. As long as we fail to see this, we cannot see where the real sin lies in our lives and end up feeling guilty over the wrong things. We fail to see that like the elder son, we, too, lie to God and to ourselves. For the elder son, in his self-righteous rancor, doesn't realize he most certainly has disobeyed his father's orders. He just did, by refusing to go in to the banquet. His rebellion takes place at home while his younger brother's took place in a foreign country. But they both rebelled.

Further, the elder brother now acts worse than his younger brother, for he accuses his father of being unjust. He got a calf, and I didn't even get a kid! The older brother can't see clearly because the slavery mentality has blinded him to the truth that he was not only free of obligations but that he was, in fact, son and heir of his father's kingdom all the while. This is much like us, who allow our guilt and shame to blind us from God's great love for us.

And now the elder brother distances himself even further, for he describes his own brother as "this son of yours." He refuses to claim him as his own brother. He hence puts himself outside his own family. Here is the ultimate result of self-righteousness, it seems to me: putting ourselves so far above the "impure" that we end up alone, on a pedestal of our own making.

But the self-righteousness is not finished. It now gets vulgar. It spells out for the father the crime of his brother: He chose whores over you and your coming old age. He has chosen not only to indulge in disgusting public wantonness, but has used your hard-earned property to do so. Another major insult is hence hurled at the father. What should the response of the father be to such an attack? Out of our self-righteousness we know only too well. But this, of course, is not the father of our self-righteousness but rather the Father of Jesus.

In gentle, tender tones and mild voice he answers his raging son:

> "My son, you are with me always, and all I have is yours.
> But it was only right we should celebrate and rejoice, because
> your brother here was dead and has come to life; he was lost
> and is found." (Lk. 15: 31-32)

There is no scolding, no anger, no condemnation for the several personal insults hurled at him. He begins with the affectionate "my son," and immediately reminds him that he owns everything that his father owns, but even more than owning, the father seems to be pointing out an ontological union that can never be broken. It is a profound declaration of love that goes far beyond gift-giving, or sharing in another's wealth: This love includes sharing in the other's very being.

And because of this union the older brother is asked, indeed pleaded with, to see the importance of a joyful celebration at the return of "your brother," who is as much a part of this family as he is. The father asks the older son to claim his brother back as brother.

It is a pleading, a sign coming out of the father's depths, a yearning for his son to see that the heart requires celebration when a part of the body that had been wounded is healed. Celebration is the only appropriate response.

And here the parable ends. Jesus clearly intended it to be yet another bridge between the grumbling Pharisees and Scribes – the self-righteous in all of us – and the God who chooses to celebrate with, rather than condemn and punish, the outcast in his midst, in our midst.

The Father of our Lord Jesus the Christ is a God of such great mercy and compassion that a return home, away from our shame-based and guilt-laden lives, becomes not only a perennial possibility but our very hope for the future. This return, if we but take the time to reflect on the implications of the parable, will be such a grand event that even the most creative amongst us will have difficulty fathoming it.

Conclusion and Summary

In this chapter I have tried to identify some of the sources of our guilt and shame. I pointed out that feelings of guilt result from violating norms that we have internalized without processing. Shame derives from feeling that we have violated the norms of significant others, and society in general. They both represent forms of fear.

I then presented Jesus' way out of these two painful states. He teaches that reconciliation occurs when we accept His invitation to a banquet that He himself hosts for the guilty and shameful. Coming to the banquet brings about acceptance and makes possible a brand new way of living, free from fear.

Finally, I illustrated the significance of accepting this invitation by offering the parable of the Prodigal Son, in which I hope a brand new way of understanding and appreciating God was delineated.

I now turn to some exercises that I trust will help us further interiorize the significance of the invitation to return home, from the distant lands where guilt and shame prevail, to the joyful celebration that awaits us at the table of reconciliation.

An Exercise for Guilt and Shame (I)

Take out a sheet of paper and make two columns, one for guilt and one for shame. Make a list of the issues or events in your life that you feel guilty about, and those that cause you to feel shame.

Become still, close your eyes if you wish, focus on your breathing. After a few moments take five deep breaths, from all the way in to all the way out.

Now, as you breathe in use a prayer word with it. (God, Jesus, peace, love, freedom, etc.) As you breathe out name the first guilt or shame item on your list, and release it with your breath.

Do this with each item on your two lists.

When you feel the peace, or the love, or the acceptance of Jesus, or God, or just a feeling of self-acceptance, then rest in that.

An Exercise for Guilt and Shame (II)

Become still. Close your eyes if you wish.

Sense Jesus walking into your room and sitting down across from you. He looks at you with great love and compassion. You tell him of the turmoil you feel over your guilts and your shame.

Hear Jesus say to you that He can take them away from you, if you wish.
"Do you trust me to do this for you?" He asks.
Do you trust Him? Even if you don't, do so now, in faith.

Jesus then gets up, comes over to you and places His hands on your head. You feel a sense of peace come over you. Rest in this peace.

Then hear Jesus say to you, "You are precious to me, you are my chosen one. Be healed."

Stay with the feelings these words generate in you. End your prayer when the feelings wane.

Guilt and Shame
(A poem for meditation)

"To thine own self be true."
Polonius

Wasn't Hannibal the Cannibal true?
Wasn't Genghis Khan? And Charles Manson
and Jeffrey Dahmer? Wasn't Hitler?

To what self must I be true?
Polonius, the old fool, gives bad advice
to his children. He dies, stabbed, lurking
behind a curtain. His daughter drowns,
trying to be true to a false suitor.
Prince Hamlet is only pretending.
Or is pretense part of his truth?

Madness, friend, may be in our blood.
We may crush the grapes
until blood flows, but
we cannot make blood from a turnip.
We cannot be what we cannot be,
though ever since the Garden
we have tried. It is not so
hard to be true to our self
once we have discovered who
we are. Find thy true self.
This is the first dictum. After that
it follows as day the night.
After that the true self
will confirm the truth.

No matter how hard
the truth, then
it will follow.

Once found,
it will lead
us to its
own
fidelity.

Reconciliation Inventory

1) The people I did not like in my childhood, and why:

2) As a child, I sought to be reconciled with those who hurt me by (list methods):

3) The people I dislike today, and why:

4) As an adult, I seek reconciliation by (list methods):

5) I feel reconciliation with them is important because:

6) I still "go to confession" because:

7) Have I celebrated the Sacrament of Reconciliation communally? If not, why not?

8) What steps can I take to celebrate Reconciliation communally in my church?

9) What have been the most effective ways I have found to be reconciled with those I have hurt, or those who may have hurt me?

10) If I am feeling wounded by someone, some situation, or event, am I willing to courageously seek help from a professional counselor, therapist, minister, priest, or a dear friend so that my healing can begin? Remember, the first step is usually the hardest! What do I see as obstacles to seeking help?

11) What do I see as the benefits of seeking help?

An Exercise for the Prodigal Son (I)

Is there someone in your family, or in your immediate circle of friends, whom you disapprove of at this time in your life? Call that person to mind.

Who is that person? Let the anger and resentment you have towards that person surface. Take your time about this. It may help to draw a picture of that person. It does not have to be flattering. Draw as you feel.

Now fantasize this person coming to you in dire straits, asking for your help.

What does he or she look like?

Are you willing to help that person?

If so, how far are you willing to go? Do you have conditions attached.

If not, what do you say to that person?

While you are visiting with your relative or friend, Jesus appears. What do you feel about His arrival at this time – opportune or inopportune timing on His part?

What does Jesus say to you about your response to your visitor and his or her request? Take your time about formulating Jesus' words for yourself. They do not need to follow any expected formula.

Listen to your feelings and thoughts on the matter for awhile.

Jesus says, "I accept you, no matter what . . . "

End your prayer when you sense that you believe in Jesus' acceptance of you.

An Exercise for the Prodigal Son (II)

You receive an invitation from a very prominent citizen to a great banquet for someone you dislike, or someone who has AIDS. In spite of your negative feelings, you decide to accept the invitation and go.

When you arrive at the banquet you find that all the prominent people in town are there. You chat with them about the guest of honor during the cocktail hour. What do you say about him or her? What do they say to you?

The guest of honor now comes over to you. He/she thanks you profusely for coming and gives you a most unexpected and lavish gift. It is the one gift you have always wanted someone to give you. He/she smiles, and leaves you to visit with the other guests.

How do you feel towards the guest of honor now. Any changes in your opinion?

An Exercise for the Prodigal Son (III)

Meditate on the parable but do so entirely from the father's perspective.

Allow the feelings of the father to become your own at each development in the story.

Do not judge yourself, just go with the flow and see what happens.

The Prodigal Son
(Poems for Meditation)

I

The Return

The father or the mother stands
with open arms. "All that I have . . ."

The lost world can never be recovered,
the children fear, approaching.

The one without shoes considers naked feet.
The one without means stands empty-handed.

No one can imagine the middle ground,
yet the loving parent steps forward,
arms open, says "All that I have . . ."

A child falls to the ground.
A child falls into the embrace,
The parent is the bridge.
"All that I have . . ."

The bridge is the possibility.
It does not guarantee we cross.
It guarantees that the crossing
is within the realm
of possibilities.

Thanks be to God
for the realm
of possibilities.

II

A Bridge

Something leaves the station in the night.
A train plods its way toward morning.
The signal flashes.
Everything happens
again and again.

III

The Bridge Again

Flesh, Mother says, is
what we are.

This hole in my middle
is the mark that I have
come from another.

This hole in my life
is the sign that I am
going to another.

Flesh, Mother says, is
what we have been.

What we will be is
not yet revealed.

When it is revealed,
we will all be
something else
anyway.

IV

Longing for Home

How she must have ached at eleven,
turning from her mother's grave, never
to return. Taking with her to the New World
the two little sisters and the baby brother,
turning their backs on the hard ground
of their blessed mother's grave, she must
have turned again to look.

She was not struck into a pillar of salt,
though it streamed down her face,
the traces of wet salt she would taste
again on the ocean when the baby brother
died, buried in the deep salt ocean,
tasted it again when she met the father
in the New World.

Her father's riches turned the earth red
with strawberries. He built movie theatres.
Her sisters married and like her bore
their many fruits into the fertile valleys
of the green world, where tears continued
to stream down their faces, maps of
wrinkles forming in their smiles.

She never spoke of that blessed grave
they'd left across the ocean.
She never returned to it.
But even spilled salt
on a table must have left
the temptation for her always
to kiss the tip of her finger,
to taste and remember
what could never
be retrieved.

Chapter III

FEAR OF PEOPLE

*L*et's look at our fear of "other" people. Most of us fear certain groups of people. This fear is known as prejudice. It is an all-too-common phenomenon, and I hope understanding its sources a little better will ameliorate the condition for us and so help alleviate the fears behind it.[1]

Webster's New World Dictionary defines prejudice as "a judgment or opinion formed before the facts are known; preconceived idea favorable or, more usually, unfavorable." This definition includes the obvious but frequently ignored aspect of prejudice that points to the fact that a prejudice can be positive as well as negative toward a person or thing. However, fears operate in negative prejudice, so let's focus on these.

Prejudice is a feeling not based on actual experience. Now, it is not easy to determine how much of a person's experience he or she will consider "actual," or personally experienced. For a prejudiced person, there will always be a claim of sufficient "actual" and, hence, personal experience. This person will tell of terrible experiences he or she had with whites, blacks, Catholics, refugees, etc. The memories of the terrible experiences are usually selective and are often mixed up with hearsay and gossip.

No one can possibly know all whites, blacks, Catholics, refugees, etc., so any negative judgment about them as a whole is an instance of thinking ill of a group without sufficient reason. It is, of course, difficult to draw the line between sufficient and insufficient reason, yet it is difficult to deny that often we form judgments on little actual information. If a person, upon receiving new information that contradicts or corrects the previous generalization, changes his or her opinion, then it would be fair to say that such a person is no longer prejudiced. As Gordon Allport says in his book, *The Nature of Prejudice*, "Prejudgments become prejudices only if they are not reversible when exposed to new knowledge."[2] The difficulty here is that a person who is prejudiced has emotion attached to that prejudice, making it difficult to change his or her opinion even after receiving new and contradictory information about the previous over-generalization. The emotions will not give way easily.

A generalized negative belief towards a group carries with it a hostile attitude toward that group, fostered, in turn, by a set of beliefs that the group has a number of objectionable qualities. These beliefs support negative attitudes, fueled by the emotional content in those attitudes. Whenever we use "they" language about groups, we are giving in to our unexamined beliefs.

The actual behavior toward the disliked group varies and has more visible and social consequences than the beliefs and the attitudes in themselves. The negative actions range from the passive to the most violent.

According to Allport, there are five degrees of prejudice, each one more intense than the former. The first level he calls antilocution. This consists of speaking against the discriminated group in one's own social circle. The second is avoidance, in which we avoid the person or group. The third is discrimination, in which active steps are taken to exclude the group. The fourth is physical attack, in which acts of violence are perpetrated against the group. The fifth is extermination, which covers lynchings, massacres, and organized mass extermination such as the tragic slaughter of the Jews in Nazi Germany. Allport notes that activity on one level of prejudice facilitates movement to the next, more intense, level.

All of us are guilty of some form of prejudice. Merely understanding where we are on this ladder can help alleviate this condition in us.

Why are we prejudiced? The initial and obvious answer is that we feel more comfortable living, playing, working, and praying with our own kind. This is true not only of major social groups but also of minorities. It is a lot of trouble attempting to assimilate foreign groups into our social circles, and the rewards for attempting to do so are not readily evident. There is also the fear that foreign groups could introduce impurities of a cultural, societal, religious, or sexual nature into our group. These fears are, of course, augmented by gossip and rumors that fuel our prevailing prejudices. Prejudices are not easily eradicated even if evidence to the contrary is presented, for the beliefs are always accompanied by the emotional dimension that maintains the irrationality.

I remember Tony deMello telling this story at a retreat:

> Some Irish laborers were working outside a house of prostitution .... Presently, the local Protestant minister comes by, turns up his collar and goes in. They say, "Did you see that? But what can you expect? Protestants!" Then came the rabbi; he turned up his collar and went in. Same response. Finally, the Catholic priest came along and did the same thing. Said Pat: "Now, it is a terrible thing. One of the girls must have taken ill."

The psychological functions of prejudice

Most of us by and large are not aware, on a conscious level, at any rate, why we are prejudiced. The reasons we invent are merely rationalizations and do not get to the source of the prejudice. In most cases, we are not aware of the psychological functions that prejudice serves in our lives. These functions are many, but Allport delineates four groups that seem to be the most common.

The first of these groups is a *reaction to frustration*. It seems to be a fact of life that our instinctive response to frustration is aggression in some form. When driving on a congested freeway one often finds a driver aggressively changing lanes to get but a few feet ahead of another, often shouting expletives at the other drivers who are as helpless as he or she is in the heavy traffic. This is the scapegoat theory in practice in which one's anger centers upon available rather than upon logical objects. When we apply this theory to prejudice we are approaching the heart of the problem.

Frustrations can cause us to be aggressive toward innocent people. This is a form of what is called *displacement*. Of course, displacement does not remove a person's frustration; the frustration continues and consequently the aggression continues and may even increase. Displacement also fails to deal with the heart of the problem, which is within the person's own life, either in insecurities, fears and anxieties, or some other sense of personal inadequacy. The driver on the congested freeway, for instance, in misdirecting his or her aggression toward other drivers, does not deal with his or her own responsibility for being late or taking that particular route at that particular time.

The second grouping involves people who have *the potential for violence.* This potential, Allport says, is central in explaining the origin of most social evils such as prejudice. Specifically, they are potentials, not necessarily realities; tendencies towards violence, not necessarily violence. That means they can happen but do not necessarily have to happen. Freud, in *Civilization and its Discontents,* regards aggression as one of the global, instinctive, steamboiler-like forces of life. He says:

"It is always possible to unite considerable numbers of men (and women) in love towards one another, so long as there are still some remaining as objects of aggressive manifestations."[3]

Freud relates the instinct toward aggression and violence to the desire to kill or destroy the object of the aggression.

The type of aggression associated with prejudice, though, is often one of displacement. It involves a type of person who does not deal with the problem realistically but rather becomes angry at the obstacle or at a substitute object. For example, after being abused by the boss at work the man comes home and kicks the dog, screams at the kids and abuses his wife. Most people have the potential for aggression and displacement. Since a potential is only latent and does not have to be used, it is possible to create inner and outer conditions that can reduce the frustration and so eliminate or reduce the aggression.[4]

Aggressive impulses are passing. They can come upon us all of a sudden and dissipate with an equal dispatch. But when they become organized collectively toward a group or a person, hatred is the result. In hatred the hater is sure that the fault lies in the object of hatred. Out-groups are often chosen over individuals for hatred because the group is an abstraction while the individual, as different as he or she may be perceived, remains like us. Hating an abstraction is different than hating individual, real people. Individuals in the hated group could even be friends of the hater, because they can be seen as exceptions to the unfavorable stereotype of the group. For instance, a prejudiced white family may have a black maid who is considered part of the family and hence not representative of "the rest of them."

Why do people hate other groups of people? Probably because of the frustrations of life, and the need for a secure place in the midst of these frustrations. It is also something we learn from the group we belong to, especially if our group unconsciously perceives itself as inadequate or insufficient in some way. A way of "protecting" the insufficiencies of the group would be to hate other groups, and so keep them from threatening the subliminally perceived insufficiencies of one's own group. Prejudice functions widely amongst groups who have a collective inferiority complex. The trouble is that it is hard to admit that we – you and I – may belong to such a group.

Allport's third grouping has to do with *sexuality*. Perhaps the most emotionally charged aspect of interracial prejudice emerges in this most personal of areas. Sex is a taboo subject not discussed in polite society and relegated to abstract rules and cultural taboos that reduce it to a place of tacit disapproval.

Allport notes that the central question allegedly is intermarriage. Since this sounds like a respectable issue, it usually becomes that aspect of sexuality that can be discussed: "I'll be friends with them but I don't want them marrying my daughter." The fact that has to be dealt with is that fear of intermarriage is really fear of dealing with the attraction for people of different color and social status that has always existed. Evidence of this is found in the millions of racially mixed people around the world. Historically, there is ample evidence of interracial liaisons that appear to have been made more attractive precisely because of their illicitness. But any admission of this in so-called polite society is taboo. So what goes on goes on in secret, whispered at odd moments and not discussed openly due to the delicacy of the issue. And the taboos persist and fuel the fires of prejudice and hatred.

The fourth and final grouping of Allport's is found amongst those who engage in *projection*. Projection is the tendency to attribute falsely to other people motives or traits that are one's own. It is a process hidden in the unconscious mind and can be seen in a very elementary form in simple jealousy. One who is jealous of another can be aware of that jealousy and recognize the potential for destructiveness in it, but when it becomes a feeling of resentment against innocent people who happen to have more than we have and we blame them for this deprivation, it becomes projection.

This need to judge and condemn other people, and so punish them, if you will, may be a personality trait that can actually be exhilarating. The "joy" it can generate restores our self-esteem as well as providing us with a physical relief from pent-up tension and frustration.

"I am not at fault, but others are totally to blame. I am good and virtuous, blameless in the eyes of God and human beings. Wow! Am I not great?" is the unspoken thought behind it.

Projection is a result of repressing all or part of a personal conflict situation. Repressed material usually has to do with fear and anxiety, greed, sexual desires, impulses to cruelty and aggression and other socially unapproved manifestations of oneself. By projecting hatred on a group or an individual one does not have to deal with the conflicts within oneself. Much prejudicial behavior involves projection on some level of the personality. All of us, more often than we care to admit, project our unresolved conflicts onto others.

In these four processes we find the ingredients for some of the irrationalities of our human nature. They do not explain by themselves our prejudices as such. This is because prejudice emerges always out of a specific context of social and cultural and religious taboos. But they do represent the infantile, repressed, defensive, aggressive and projective aspects of our unconscious life that can be fostered by our "culture." They must be looked at seriously if we are to live and love as maturing Christians.

Tony deMello once wrote:

"The truth that sets us free, we don't want to hear. So when we say it isn't true, what we mean is, 'I don't like it.'"[5]

Religion and prejudice

There seem to be some curious connections between religion and prejudice. The basic finding in both the U.S. and Britain is that church members tend to be more prejudiced than non-members. But this is not synonymous with church attendance. A number of studies have found that those who attend church infrequently are the most prejudiced while those who attend regularly have a low level of prejudice. Atheists and those who have no religious affiliation are the least prejudiced.[6]

This may be due to the fact that many church members belong to their church because it is a safe, powerful, superior in-group – though they may not be aware of this motivation at a conscious level. They are likely to be authoritarian and self-righteous and tempted toward prejudice. These people find a communal solidarity in their church membership that serves non-religious ends, hence they utilize church membership more as a means of feeling "safe" than of worshiping or serving God. On the other hand, those who see church membership as an end in itself – because of the teachings of the religion – have made these teachings an intrinsic part of their lives. These people see their religious beliefs as the driving force behind their lives. The studies done on this phenomenon have revealed that no more than 35 percent of church members could be classed in this latter group, while the remainder use religion for their own ends.[7]

Why do those believing in a religion and participating in it appear, in the main, to be more prejudiced than the irreligious? A key reason is that religion stands for more than faith; it is the pivot of the cultural ways of a people and no matter the initial teachings of its founder, all religions rapidly become secularized. Christianity is so much a part of Western civilization that its Jewish and essentially Eastern way of looking at reality has been all but lost. Any visitation by an out-group then is seen as a potential threat to an entire way of life.

But even more at the heart of the matter is the nature of religion itself. Any faith that teaches absolute truths and claims divine origin and approval of its teachings will naturally be in conflict with anyone who does not agree with it. Hence, by its very nature religion tends to breed prejudice toward out-groups. For instance, any authentic union among Christian denominations is unlikely as long as Catholicism believes that Protestant denominations are in error. But to change this belief is unthinkable because the very nature of Catholicism would then be threatened.

Tony deMello once said:

"Our religious convictions bear as much relation to personal holiness as a dinner jacket to digestion." How true!

A religion's influence on prejudice is paradoxical. Nearly all religions teach love of neighbor and proclaim universal truth, but all religions have practiced violence in the name of these same ideals. Religions, then, make prejudice happen even while preaching against it.

How do we respond to prejudice in our lives in the light of the God image Jesus revealed to us? By doing our best to become like this God, whom Jesus so loves and reveres. And, we must remind ourselves that this God, so generous in compassion and mercy, chose to overcome our fears by hosting a banquet for us.

We should respond accordingly, it seems to me, by hosting a banquet for the neighbor we may feel prejudiced toward in any way. I believe civil rights laws are essential for human justice to become more just toward out-groups, but laws will not change people's hearts, only their external behavior. Changing hearts occur only when in-groups and out-groups meet one another – one by one, couple by couple – in social settings. As long as we keep members of an out-group at arm's length socially, there is little hope for prejudice abating in any society. And what better place to initiate such social gatherings than at the table of the Lord? Meeting in church, and socializing there after worship with persons different from ourselves, can become the catalyzer from which friendships can develop and barriers that divide people can fall.

In order to initiate such gatherings, though, it is very important to first check in with ourselves, and ask ourselves whether we are truly open to becoming God-like in our lives or whether our God is still too small to make room for our neighbor.

Prejudice against women and children

While prejudice against out-groups is a well-known fact in society, there is another form of prejudice that has only recently been publicized. This is prejudice against women and children. Religions have again fostered this prejudice while at the same time condemning it. As a counselor, I have been startled all too frequently by both men and women who attempt to justify the physical abuse of the woman by citing scripture. Saying that such abuse is sanctioned in the Bible, they quote St. Paul:

"...As Christ is head of the Church and saves the whole body, so is a husband the head of his wife; and as the Church is subject to Christ, so should wives be to their husbands, in everything." (Eph. 5:24-25)

Women, and some men, are abused far more frequently than we may think. It often goes on behind closed doors and when it happens in public it is ignored as an occurrence that is none of our business.

Many abused women, in fact, are not aware that they are being abused, usually due to very poor self-concepts, and consequently do nothing about it.

There are warning signs, however, that can alert such women to the truth. A column by Ann Landers reflects what I believe to be very significant warning signs that must be attended to if one feels in any way abused in a relationship. These include:

1) Jealousy of your time spent away from your partner due to your need to visit family, friends and co-workers.

2) Controlling your life by making decisions for you, usually "for your own good." This includes preventing you from having your own financial resources.

3) Blaming you for his or her problems. It is all your fault.

4) Gets very upset when asked to help with work that is considered "your department."

5) Cruelty toward children, other subordinates, and animals. (Displacement is at work here and is always justified by the abuser as "necessary discipline" of the victim.)

6) Sex becomes violent and demanding and non-consensual.

7) Verbal abuse, either regularly or infrequently, but always directed at your ineptness, inadequacies, or unapproved-of behavior.

8) Sudden mood swings that alternate between being very loving and very angry in a short period of time.

9) Breaking or striking objects, pounding the table with his

or her fists, throwing objects across the room close to you but not hitting you.

10) Uses force, like hitting you, choking you, stabbing or shooting you during an argument.

These are some of the symptoms to look out for if you suspect you may be a victim of abuse. Identifying the warning signs is the first step; the second is seeking help as soon as possible. Often, tomorrow is too late.

Once I was visiting with a young widow who had been treated harshly from the day she was born. She had been abused throughout her childhood by her several adoptive parents and had characteristically married an abusive man who regularly put her down verbally, physically and sexually. She gave birth to two sons who, encouraged by their father, frequently yelled at her and derided her even when they were children. In their adolescent years they ignored her in her attempts to discipline them. Then, all of a sudden, her husband died. After the funeral she found out that her husband had given the house and all the property to his sons, leaving her with nothing. The sons informed her they would let her continue to live in the house but proceeded to make her life hell.

Pain was etched into her face as she looked at me and said, "It seems I was born to be adopted and alone. What should I do?" I was so absorbed in the injustice of it all, I just shook my head at her question. After awhile I said, "What do you think will be best for you?" She answered, not surprisingly, "I don't know." She had never considered what was best for her in her entire life so I was not surprised she did not know what would be best for her now. Together then we started exploring various options that would establish her independence from her sons and provide her with a life of dignity and respect elsewhere. This, I believe, is very important to do with abused people. And it is very hard. But, I believe, it is essential that it be done as a first step toward recovery and healing.

Of course, millions of children are routinely abused by their parents or other adults in their young lives as well, often in the name of discipline or punishment. This abuse is well-documented in the media, both through news reports and through shows developed for entertainment purposes, such as real-life dramas and movies.

Andrew Vachss, an attorney who has devoted much of his life to protecting children, in a disturbing article on emotional child abuse, defines emotional abuse as the systematic diminishment of another.[8] It may be intentional, subconscious, or both. It is designed to reduce a child's self-concept to the point where the victim considers himself or herself unworthy – unworthy of respect, unworthy of friendship, unworthy of the natural birthright of all children, namely, love and protection. Vachss observes that emotional abuse can be verbal or behavioral, active or passive, frequent or occasional. Regardless, it is often as painful as physical assault.

From my own practice, I have found that children, women and men who have been abused, and some who continue to be abused, have one thing in common: They have very poor self-concepts and feel guilty over anything and everything. Indeed one gets the impression they feel guilty for being alive. This, of course, is not surprising since that is the message they have received from their abusers, sometimes for years. The abused person is steeped in fear. As May Sarton, a pioneer in women's rights, has written, "Suffering often feels like failure," and the more one suffers the more one feels like a failure. And feeling like a failure breeds feelings of fear.

It is essential, therefore, that the abused person seek professional help. This is very hard for them to do because, of course, they don't feel they deserve or need it. But they, above all people, certainly do. As Sarton observes, we fear bringing to light what is painful, for that may initiate change, disturb our private hell – which is so often preferred to the liberation that revealing our tragic circumstances to another can bring about. This is where the lie operates and indeed serves as the perpetuator of the abuse.

It is also very important that the victim set up his or her own private system of values, one's own standards of what is right and wrong. Vachss calls this *self-referencing.* I suggest this begins with recognizing the lie one has been living, and claim this truth: that every person has the right to be respected, and no one has the right to take that away from another. No one. There is no room whatsoever for any human being to abuse another, either physically, emotionally, sexually or socially. Yet it goes on, and the perpetrators come from all walks of life, from the ghettoes all the way up the social ladder to the very rich. Abuse is an equal opportunity employer. It is one of the consequences of prejudice.

What goes for emotional abuse obviously goes for physical and sexual abuse as well. Once I was listening to a woman in her mid-thirties who had just been severely abused, verbally and physically, by her husband. She had bruises, her wrist was in a brace, and she hurt all over. He had demanded sex from her while in a drunken state; she refused, and he beat her. If a neighbor had not come by, she said, he probably would have killed her. She swore she would never go back to him. This had happened several times before, and she always went back after a few days. She had once consulted a priest, who urged her to go back, asserting that she had an obligation to do so. He obviously didn't know better, nor know her situation. Her self-concept was so poor that she listened to him and did go back, and was beaten even more severely again in a few days. The cycle of violence can be broken only if she is open to hearing words of self-affirmation, words of self-respect. With me, she spoke strongly, assuring me she was not going back, ever. It was then that the phone rang. It was her husband. He told her he knew where she was and, in fact, had come and taken her car that was parked outside my office. She would have to walk back to her girlfriend's house, he said.

The helpless feeling one has when one is stalked came over me at that time, as well. I urged her to call the police. She refused. She argued that the car was community property, that he had a right to take it, and so on. She was the victim again, no matter her earlier protestations of never returning to him. When she left, in spite of her continuing assertions that she would never return to him, I felt it was a matter of time before she did.

Prejudice against the weak by the strong is contrary to the entire message of the Gospel of Jesus Christ. It is absolutely not God's way, as we have seen, and must not be fostered or supported or encouraged in any way by anyone, under any circumstances. And anyone who is being abused – physically, emotionally, sexually, or any other way – has an obligation to get out of the situation and never return to it. As believers in Jesus, it is our obligation, I believe, to reach out to the victim and offer a hand of compassion and love, and not withdraw it until that victim has been rendered safe, until he or she allows love, our love, to transcend his or her fears. This could take time, for the victims usually believe they ought to be punished for their behavior; they have been told so, usually in no uncertain terms, by the abuser. Changing a potentially life-threatening situation is therefore not seen as an option by the victim; and death, either spiritual, psychological or physical, is sometimes actually preferred by the victim, as a "just" punishment for their behavior.

While processing these thoughts, I was watching a program on television and was struck by a line I heard that seems to fit this discussion quite well. The program was describing animal behavior in times of severe, life-threatening drought in Venezuela. The animals would migrate, sometimes great distances, far away from their familiar surroundings, in search of water. Some would make it, others would not, but the instinct for survival was so strong they tried anyway. The narrator concluded by observing that "accepting change is neither good nor bad; it is a question of survival." How true, and how sad, that so many human beings, because of prior conditioning and indoctrination, allow their fear of change to override their natural instincts for survival, dying metaphorically or literally in the process.

We all have some fear of certain individuals or groups of people. Some of these fears are rational but quite a few of them are not. I believe that if we take our faith in Jesus seriously we must take practical steps to rid ourselves of these irrational fears. This means seeing a counselor of some kind, attending therapeutic group sessions, seeking legal counsel if need be, calling on friends for support and protection, and so on. But, we must *do* something because living in fear of others, whatever the reasons, is not healthy, and certainly does not represent the call of Jesus to see, deep within our hearts, a daughter or son of God, free beyond all measure.

A liberating way of Jesus:
The Widow and the Judge

One of the finest examples of the importance of taking the initiative in changing one's lot in life when it becomes unbearable, and possibly life-threatening, is the parable of the widow and the judge. In it Jesus makes very clear the appropriate Christian response for such a situation.

In the parable, Jesus is speaking of the importance of persistence in prayer. I suggest that prayer here involves not merely praying to God for liberation sometime in the future but recognizing God already at work, liberating us in the midst of our difficulties, through other people, and through the events of our days. The emerging courage we may sense within us right now, enabling us to overcome our current fears and ensuing paralysis, is the grace of God, yearning that we hear, understand, and act to change our lots in life that may have become unbearable.

Let us take a closer look at this parable to find in it the challenge to reduce our fear of other people and concomitantly claim our rights as unique individuals.

> Then he told them a parable about the need to pray continually and never lose heart. "There was a judge in a certain town," he said, "who had neither fear of God nor respect for anyone." (Lk. 18: 1-2)

The parable opens by depicting a judge who is described, in Western translations, as one who neither fears God nor respects men or women. Bailey notes that in all the Middle Eastern translations, the judge is described as someone who is not ashamed before people, meaning someone unable even to be aware of the evil of his actions in the presence of one who should make him ashamed, the destitute widow. In a shame-based society, as in the Middle East, not feeling shame before people is one of the harshest criticisms possible. In this instance shame means honest humility and does not represent a negative state of self-doubt as discussed earlier. Abusers usually lack this humility. The judge also has no fear of God, meaning he has no guilt feelings either, no inner sense of right and wrong, no conscience. Abusers usually have a warped sense of right and wrong.

> In the same town there was also a widow who kept on coming
> to him and saying, "I want justice from you against my enemy!"
> (Lk. 18:3)

Before this kind of man comes a widow. The widow is a symbol of the weak and the powerless, a true victim. In Middle Eastern society, the sad state of widows was well known, for they had no one to protect them and no money to buy that protection. In fact, widows were often exploited, victims of injustice and ill treatment. It may be helpful to note that widows, by and large, were not old women, aged and infirm. In a culture with a short life span, as in First Century Palestine, women who had married in their early teens often became young and vigorous widows. Further, in spite of their ill treatment they did have some rights in the Jewish legal tradition, based on Isaiah 1:17, which said:

> Take your wrong-doing out of my sight.
> Cease to do evil.
> Learn to do good,
> search for justice,
> help the oppressed,
> be just to the orphan,
> plead for the widow.

Next to orphans, therefore, widows were to be listened to and helped. Of course, this particular widow is up against a judge who cared not a whit for the widow's rights, no matter from where those rights derived.

This widow asserts herself boldly in a very hostile environment. The judge would have been sitting comfortably on a raised platform, in an open courtyard crowded with men. He had several of his legal assistants on either side of him, men who not only gave him counsel but also collected the bribes from hopeful litigants. The larger the bribe, the better the chance of an individual's case being heard early, and the better the chance for a favorable outcome of the case.

Women, furthermore, did not even belong in court; it was a man's world. Her presence there meant she was truly alone in the world with no man around, even from her own family, willing to go to court for her.

Now, this woman kept on coming to him demanding justice.

She did not just try once, not twice, but over and over again, day after day. Bailey points out that her cry is a call for justice and protection, not vengeance.[9] Jeremias observes that the issue at hand would appear to be a money matter: a debt, or a portion of her inheritance being withheld from her, probably by a relative, possibly her own son.[10] If this were a withholding of her inheritance – and the Greek suggests a male adversary, making this conclusion likely – her situation was dire indeed. The portion set aside for her after her husband's death was all she had a right to claim. Not receiving it would amount to a life-and-death situation: She would be faced with poverty, starvation, or a life of prostitution, if denied her rights. Nevertheless, the shock of the parable is found here, that she came out, day after day, and publicly demanded her rights, shouting out over the din of all the other male litigants, without resorting to bribery, just crying out, over and over again, day after day.

All she had going for her was her persistence. And for a long time it looked bad for her, for the scripture says, "For a long time he refused." Knowing what kind of a man we are dealing with, of course, this is not surprising. What is surprising, though, is the judge's soliloquy. In case we have forgotten, he begins it by affirming rather haughtily that he indeed is someone who neither fears God nor respects man (or woman).

> For a long time he refused, but at last he said to himself, "Even though I have neither fear of God nor respect for any human person, I must give this widow her just rights since she keeps pestering me, or she will come and slap me in the face." (Lk. 18: 4-5)

The words used in this translation, "slap me in the face," do not really capture the judge's meaning. The phrase is actually a term taken from boxing, a prize fighter's term, Bailey notes, and means receiving "a blow under the eye."[11] It is really very humorous to hear the judge say this as the reason for vindicating her. After all, here we have a man filled with his own importance, who could not care less for God or people, an original "fat cat," if you will, surrounded by all his cronies, and well protected by them, no doubt. And he gives in to a helpless widow because he fears she may beat him up! She is hardly in a position to even get close to him, let alone give him a black eye. Yet, this is what he fears in giving in to her. It is clearly an exaggeration on the judge's part, intended to communicate how much her persistence has upset him. This persistence, in the Greek, implies a strong wish to go on and on, like forever! The judge does not want to risk this; she has already given him a headache, so he gives in.

Persistence in prayer is clearly the main point of the parable, but I suggest the very setting Jesus uses invites us to a broader understanding of prayer that involves demanding our rights – even before hopeless odds, even though out of our element, even though we may feel shouted down by the crowd who wish we would go away and not come back. If the unjust judge heard her cries, how much more will God, the truly righteous One, hear ours.

Fear of other people, especially those who threaten us in any way, those who wield a power of some sort over us, must not keep us from demanding our right to live. We must also realize that giving in to fear of other people, either as groups or individuals, makes it impossible for us to reach out to them in love. And because our Creator has reached out to us first, we must at least try to move out of ourselves toward our sisters and brothers as a thanksgiving response to our God. This movement, if practiced by Christians of all denominations, everywhere, can literally melt prejudices, and bring us all nearer to the "Kingdom of God."

In a contemporary world, not so far removed from Jesus' day in matters of injustice and abuse, it is very hard for certain people who have been abused throughout their lives to cry out for justice persistently. This is because such people have very low self-concepts. They have come to believe they deserve the injustice given them, and fear that demanding their rights will simply intensify the injustice. "Keep quiet, don't say anything, don't make any trouble, and then maybe things will get better," they say to themselves. Of course, "things" do not get better. Convincing such persons to take the initiative to change their lot in life is very difficult.

They need love, support and affirmation after affirmation of their own worthwhileness. The lie they have been living must be confronted and sent away, the lie that states he or she is a no-body, unworthy of anyone's attention, let alone love. The abused person must be helped to see the truth: his or her own beauty, uniqueness and goodness. The widow in the parable stands out as a powerful sign to all such people to do what has to be done in changing one's lot in life if injustice and abuse are occurring.

Fear of other people who try to assert their power over us, by looking down on us individually or collectively (as in social preju-dice), ought not keep us from asserting our rights before them. In fact, as we have seen in the parable of the widow and the judge, God expects us to demand our rights, over and over again, in conjunction with asking God, over and over again, to give us the courage and the wisdom we need to persevere in asserting ourselves and our cause before those who seek to destroy our significance as God's own daughters and sons.

Let us now turn to some exercises that I pray will help you interiorize further the words you have just read.

The Prejudice Inventory

1)   I fear people who...

2)   As a result of my fear, I look upon these people as...

3)   I am prejudiced against (name group or individuals) because...

4)   I am willing/not willing to change my opinion toward them because...

5)   I have consciously discriminated against (name group or individuals) because...

6)   I have participated in acts of violence actively/passively against (name group or individuals) because...

7)   I include/exclude (name group or individuals) from my social circle because...

8)   I express my frustrations by:

9)   I feel aggressive toward (name group or individuals) when I am feeling...

10)   I have been sexually attracted/not attracted toward (name group or individuals) at these times in my life:

11)   The consequences of this for me have been:

12)   In regard to the above item, I have thrown the blame on:

13)   My religious beliefs/practices have affected my prejudices by:

14)   I see myself religiously as intrinsic/extrinsic because...
The reasons for this are:

15)   I am willing/not willing to initiate social gatherings at church with (name group or individuals) because I believe/do not believe it makes me more God-like.

16)   I see women/men in my life as:

17)   Children are important/not important to me because:

18)   I am willing to act/not act when I suspect abuse is going on in my neighborhood because:

An Exercise for the Widow and the Judge (I)

Sense that you are in a position of authority over someone, or over several people. Picture a scene where you are actually wielding this authority either behind a desk, or in a classroom, or in a jail as a guard, or even as a judge in a courthouse.

The "subordinate" comes before you with an outrageous request. You reject it out of hand.

A few days later the "subordinate" returns with the same outrageous request. Again you reject it.

This happen several times.

Do you ever give in? Remember, there is no rational reason to do so, and your position will not be jeopardized if you do.

Now, Jesus is brought before you. Imagine He is also your "subordinate." He makes the same outrageous request. What do you do?

Listen to your feelings, your justifications.

Jesus tells you, "My Father's Kingdom will be furthered if you give in to my request." Do you still resist?

What will it take for you to change your mind and give in to the outrageous request?

An Exercise for the Widow and the Judge (II)

You receive a telephone call informing you that you have just lost everything you own. You are destitute.

Devastated, you call several of your friends to tell them the news, and to ask them for their help.

Every single one of them refuses to help you, and asks you not to call them again.

Listen to your feelings and thoughts as you are rejected.

You decide to make one more telephone call. You pick up the telephone and the line is dead. Your telephone has been disconnected.

What do you do now? Are there any avenues left open for you? There are none.

Jesus suddenly presents Himself to you. What does He say to you? What do you say to Him?

Attend to the dialogue with an open heart and mind.

Jesus offers you a solution, but it involves public humiliation. Do you accept his solution or look for another.

Jesus says this is the only way you can become well again. Do you believe Him?

Are you willing to fight for justice? For yourself? For a neighbor?

An Exercise for the Widow and the Judge (III)

Meditate on the parable from the point of view of the judge. Become the judge . . . feel his power . . . feel his succumbing to her incessant demands.

Meditate then from the point of view of the widow. Become the widow . . . feel her desperation . . . her powerlessness . . . her eventual success.

What have you learned about yourself and your relationship with God through this prayer exercise?

Chapter IV

FEAR OF LONELINESS

*O*ne of the great fears of modern society is the fear of loneliness or alienation. This is the most personal of fears, for it affects us in the very pit of our stomachs.

It has been described and defined by many contemporary scholars in various ways, but fear of loneliness is such a commonly experienced fear among human beings that clinical definitions and prosaic descriptions often appear so objective and cold as to have little impact on our guts, and often appear irrelevant.

Loneliness hurts. The pain is not just psychological; it often can manifest itself through physical symptoms that refuse to go away. We feel hollow inside, we feel empty at our core, we feel worthless, much like T.S. Eliot's "stuffed men" and women, filled with nothing but straw.

> We are the hollow men
> We are the stuffed men
> Leaning together
> Headpiece filled with straw. Alas![1]

Hollow people feel they have no foundation, nothing to build their lives upon. They feel that no one, above all no *one,* cares for them.

The sense of isolation makes us feel so fearful at times that we are willing to do anything to break out of it, to re-connect in any way, however unsatisfactory, with people. Dr. David Duncombe – a minister, psychologist of religion, and my former professor at Yale and Berkeley – once told me that he knew men in jail who were there because they needed the companionship.

But, alas! We often re-connect, it seems, only with people equally lonely, equally isolated and empty within, and we realize that we are but leaning on just another person of straw, for when we converse with them it is like Eliot's "wind in dry grass" or "rats' feet over broken glass, quiet and meaningless." And we fear, we fear terribly, that we will be remembered, if at all, only as "the hollow men..., the stuffed men."

The human being is a social being. We are brought up within a family unit beginning with the nurturing of our parents. We grow up relating to and with other people – relatives of our extended family, friends, lovers, mates, business associates, professional colleagues, and so on. They form our self-definitions and they tell us who we are, and enable us to discover our own uniqueness. When these external stimuli cease, or are reduced in intensity, our senses – and through them our "heart" – become lost, rudderless, on what appears to be a mighty ocean called life. Hopelessness and despair can result.

Loneliness has affected all of us at some time or another in our lives. In fact, it appears that loneliness in the modern world has reached epidemic proportions – in spite of telephones, the easy accessibility of air travel, fax machines and television. Loneliness affects the elderly, as well as the young, the wealthy industrialist, as well as the homeless woman begging on the busy street corner. It affects the coupled as well as the single, the newly wedded as well as the widower and widowed.

It is found in the story of the 90-year-old man sent to a nursing home. He shakes his head wearily and says, "One father is enough for 20 children, but 20 children are not enough to take care of one father." He sits alone, sadly, in a modern old-age home, unaware that his wife is dead. His family has never told him of Fanny's death, and he still questions God as to why she has deserted him and why she has never come home again. (Herb Goro, *New York*, Jan. 10, 1972).

It is found also among young adults. Some years ago I was a teacher and counselor at a small college. It was on the day school closed for the Christmas holidays. I was busily correcting students' papers when the phone rang. It was one of my students. She asked me whether I could come over immediately to the men's dorm where her boyfriend lived, and she said she would meet me there because there was something wrong with him. She was frantic. I went over and found him in what seemed like a catatonic trance, rocking back and forth, tears streaming down his cheeks with a glazed, unseeing look in his eyes. I tried speaking to him but there was no response. I asked her what happened. She said he had received a note that morning from his father with a check enclosed. It informed him that he was leaving for Paris with his mistress for Christmas, so that no one would be home when he arrived in Boston for the holidays. His father suggested he therefore not come home but use the check, which was left blank, to do "whatever" over the holidays.

I had been seeing this young man for counseling, had known about the traumas he had endured over the school term with his parents' divorce, and realized this letter, this rejection, and at this time, was the last straw. We got him to a hospital where he stayed for more than three weeks recovering. Merry Christmas indeed!

Loneliness is about an unrequited deep longing within all of us for a home. A home is a place where we can always go back to, a safe and secure oasis in the often harsh desert landscape of life. It is about a yearning for love. And love is all about being accepted by another or others for *who* we are, not for what the other or others think we ought to be. Divorce and breakup of relationships often occur because one partner demands that the other change before he or she will be accepted. That, of course, is not love; it is manipulation and bribery. True love accepts the beloved just as he or she is, with all warts, blemishes and rolls of fat intact. True love asks nothing from the beloved except that the love be accepted, and cherished. It can be hoped, but not demanded, that love given be returned.

Varieties of loneliness

Loneliness, and a sense of alienation, I believe, comes in a variety pack. It is not one single reality, although the ensuing feelings can be very similar. The varieties I know are these:

1) Existential loneliness
2) Loneliness emerging from the loss of a loved one through death
3) Loneliness associated with separation or divorce
4) Social alienation.

I'll try to describe these as one who has experienced them personally and with others.

Existential loneliness has to do with a loss of meaning in some significant aspect of one's life. For some years, for instance, I believed that religious institutions existed primarily for the proclamation of God's good news of salvation to those most in need of hearing it: the poor, the divorced, the widowed, and the emotionally destitute. Then I gradually came to believe that religious institutions were more about self-perpetuation than gospel; this temporary loss of meaning made me very lonely, alienated from what was the source of my hope and meaning for so long.

I had to do some very intense praying; I sought spiritual direction and counseling. Before peace and a sense of joy could emerge I had to work hard at re-defining what truly provided a meaning for my existence. I then came to recognize my own blindness, my own unrealistic expectations, and started to appreciate in a new way the many good works these institutions do, the many poor people they do indeed help, and the fact that my loss of meaning was *coming from within me.* I realized that it was only by returning to my center, to my Source of Truth, that new meaning could emerge for me. My perspective, therefore, had to change, and as it changed I found the existential loneliness of my past perceptions diminishing, and indeed being transformed into a new meaning and purpose for existence. Of course, most of us are willing to change not because we see the light but because we feel the heat!

Tragically, there are those of us who allow existential loneliness to consume us, who even after feeling the heat refuse to let go of the fire, the sources of our loneliness, and die, in some way or another. Many years ago I was deeply moved by Victor Frankl's account of life in a concentration camp. He discovered hope and, in fact, a reason to live, when prisoners around him were choosing to lie down and die. He found his reasons in the memory of the love he had shared with his wife. The fact that she had long since been executed – even though he didn't know it – didn't matter. What mattered, what gave him meaning to live, when dying was being chosen all around him, was the love he still carried in his heart, a love that made it possible for him to transcend ultimate human misery.

I believe existential loneliness can be transformed into a new sense of union only through the power of love when we allow its nurturing to touch our very souls, our inmost selves. Then the fire that can consume can become the fire that heals and brings forth new life.

But how do we allow the power of love to transform us? I believe prayer helps, experiencing in solitude the presence of the living God within us. But prayer is not enough. We must choose to step out of our isolation and reach out for companionship and understanding. This may involve attending local grief groups, or starting one's own group, or seeing a spiritual director or counselor in one's area. It may involve taking trips with singles groups or attending church functions. But whatever we do, we must take the initial step to find in our own particular environment a reason to live. In other words, while activities may help, what really transforms is something that can make us enthusiastic again. Find that something, and it will give new meaning and purpose to our existence. Then, existential loneliness can become a thing of the past for us.

Loneliness emerging from the loss of a loved one through death: Death ends not only life but love as we have known it. The love continues after death but it will never again be the same. In modern Western society we try to anesthetize ourselves against death, from our language ("She passed on.") to our funerals (in parlors and not at home). Yet the devastating loneliness emerging out of the loss of a loved one cannot be avoided. It comes after the initial shock and the ensuing numbness; the terrible pain of loneliness, it comes.

Our faith in God, in life after death, helps us, but it does not take away the pain of loneliness. No one escapes this pain, and hence everyone carries a fear within them of the day when the inevitable loss of a loved one will occur.

Fear of the grieving process is quite normal, of course. Grief entered into can be a great catharsis, because it allows a new quality of compassion to emerge, a sensitivity for others' suffering.

My focus is not so much on the grieving process, however, as on the fear of loneliness it can generate. Many excellent works have been written on the grieving process itself; they help us understand the stages we have to go through. These books can affirm us when we think we may be going crazy. But what I want to emphasize is that fear of loneliness in the process is not only normal, and to be accepted as such, but that this fear can be eventually transformed through love into a positive force for a new way of living.

I belonged to a grief group for about a year. I found in it acceptance, understanding and affirmation. It gave me the strength and the hope I needed to go on. And since everyone in the group was grieving, our empathy for one another could not help but be genuine. We had no pious platitudes, no words of wisdom, no rationalization, only a listening compassion as each person spoke, and warm, caring embraces when the tears flowed. This is what enables the loneliness to be transformed into hope that there is a future, albeit a wholly different type of future, after a death in one's life.

It is very important, I believe, that we not try to take away the fear of loneliness from the grieving brother or sister. That fear will melt the more we are *there* for the person. And being there for the person is more important than what we say or do for them. If we need to say something, "I'm sorry" will suffice. This will convey our desire to enter into the person's pain. He or she will feel the concern in those words, and be consoled. Often, though, we wonder what to say to someone who is sobbing uncontrollably. What we must remember is that there is nothing to say. There are no words that will "fix it" because there is nothing to fix. What the grieving person needs more than anything else is our presence; this will be the balm for healing.

I have found that people in the midst of their initial grieving have people around them. But after a few weeks we tend to abandon the griever. It is precisely during the weeks or months after the funeral, though, that the loneliness intensifies and the griever needs other people around, to support and comfort him or her – not to take the loneliness away but to *be there* while he or she is feeling lonely. Often, we forget to do this, and if we remember, perhaps our own fear of one day being abandoned prevents us from visiting or even telephoning. Yet I suggest that this time is as important a time to be with the griever as was the time right after the death. Being there is how love can help transcend the fear, can bring life out of death. If each one of us remembers to do this, the next time we are with a grieving brother or sister, we can be assured that when our time to grieve comes, the weeks and the months after our bereavement will not be without friends, though it will be lonely.

Loneliness associated with separation or divorce: The loneliness that flows over us like red hot volcanic lava as the result of the rupturing of a love relationship seems to occur as suddenly as the eruption of a volcano. Even though rumblings were probably present before the eruption, these breakups always seem unexpected. They can devastate an individual.

I was discussing the trauma with an old friend of mine who had been through it several years ago. She told me the anguish she went through immediately after her husband left. It was indescribable: uncontrollable tears day and night, loss of appetite, a need to throw a huge "pity party" alone or with others, and a desperate reaching out to friends or even acquaintances for solace. And nothing seemed to help. The feelings of abandonment were at times overwhelming, the sense of futility, crushing.

This loneliness compels some individuals, depending on the personality, to isolate themselves; it prompts others to engage in promiscuity. Both are coping mechanisms that do not ultimately satisfy; they do not take the pain away. The jumbled thoughts, ranging from seeking vengeance to a forlorn hope that maybe the beloved will return, do not really help and, in fact, could make things worse by holding out a false hope. For some women, especially in patriarchal and less educated societies, "the myth of the male" makes matters even worse, for the belief among these women, that without a man she is nothing, prevails and serves to exacerbate the loneliness.

There is one point, however, that I believe is important: There is no longer any fear of abandonment; there *is* abandonment. And this means the only way out is up, because one is already at the very bottom! This fact, once realized, can bring with it a ray of hope.

The sufferer has to force herself or himself to act. Friends help, counseling helps, and prayer helps. It is also very helpful if the sufferer has previously developed a system of inner convictions about herself or himself. It is called faith, in God, as well as in one's own intrinsic worth.

Much of the later suffering – meaning the suffering that follows the initial shock – is due to a new wave of fear that tries to convince the sufferer that life is dangerous and threatening and that "no one is out there for me." With this feeling comes the exaggerated fear that all one has believed in is a lie, that nothing really offers an ultimate meaning. This is why it is very important to seek help, professional or otherwise, so that "reality checks" can be built in to the sufferer's recovery process.

And we can recover; in fact, most of us do. While this may appear impossible at the time, it does happen, more often than not, and we become better human beings for it, more compassionate, more sensitive, more understanding and patient with others than ever before. This is because we have been there, we know what it is like "from the inside."

For years, I have been inspired by the following passage, which I feel would be an appropriate way to end this section:

After A While

After a while you learn the subtle difference
    between holding a hand and chaining a soul,
and you learn that love doesn't mean leaning
    and company doesn't always mean security,
and you begin to learn that kisses aren't contracts
    and presents aren't promises,
and you begin to accept your defeats with your head up
    and your eyes ahead,
    with the grace of a woman, not the grief of a child.
And you learn to build all your roads on today because
    tomorrow's ground is too uncertain for plans,
    and futures have a way of falling down in mid-flight.
After a while you learn that even sunshine burns
    if you get too much.
So you plant your own garden and decorate your own soul,
instead of waiting for someone to bring you flowers.
And you learn that you really can endure,
you really are strong, you really do have worth.
And you learn and you learn,
with every goodbye, you learn...

–Veronica A. Shoffstall

Social alienation: We receive our idea of who we are through other people. Beginning with our parents and our early relationships, they tell us what kind of a person we are. This information continues coming to us through adolescence and adulthood. Other people define us, and we often allow our lives to be fashioned by these definitions.

The "misfits" of society are often thought to be the ones who rebel against these definitions, the ones who "do their own thing." These are judged to be leaders, revolutionaries, saints or criminals, depending on the extent of the boundaries of society they shatter, and on society's perceptions of that extent.

Most people, however, do not shatter society's boundaries, and the reason is fear. Fears of being rejected by the society we inhabit, anxieties over losing position and prestige, concerns over rattling the cages of our relatives and friends, all of these things preclude unacceptable social behavior. The fear ultimately is the fear of alienating oneself from others, from being left lonely and isolated from the rest of humanity.

In a contemporary world, however, conforming to social expectations does not seem to be enough. We still feel isolated. We still feel lonely. A fear of this loneliness pervading our whole life emerges. Why is this?

In a few short years in our evolutionary history as human beings, society has changed drastically. Modern conveniences, for instance, that we now take for granted, did not exist a half century ago. Easy air travel, cellular phones, VCRs, and microwave ovens, while making life easy also make life difficult. They take away the need for leisurely social communion with one another. We are always on the go, busy, very busy, with deals and with contracts, but paradoxically also very lonely, and isolated. At odd moments, we may pause and ask ourselves, "What's it all about," but then we have no time to wait for the answer that can emerge only if we give it time to emerge. And time appears always to be in short supply.

Until recent times, this life on the run belonged chiefly to the man of the house. It now belongs to the woman, as well. Robert Wright, in his informative essay "The Evolution of Despair," notes that suburban living of the 1950s was particularly hard on women with young children.[2] In previous ages, where the extended family, even the whole village, took charge of child rearing, the isolation of the suburban housewife did not exist. But in modern society "the quiet desperation, the anger and despair" that feminist leader Betty Friedan called "the problem with no name" led to women rebelling against their confinement and exchanging their aprons for business suits.

As a result, men and women, both working long hours in different places, rarely see each other, let alone have leisure time together. And the children become incidental, and alone, and afraid, and develop their own defense mechanisms for survival: drugs, sex, alcohol, violence, television. All these survival mechanisms have one thing in common: They isolate; they do not allow intimacy to evolve. The fear of being alone becomes anesthetized through the mechanisms; the fear, however, although repressed, remains as anxiety.

The solution of genuine community

According to evolutionary psychology, the problem with modern society is less that we're "oversocialized" than that we're undersocialized – or, that too little of our social contact is social in the natural, intimate sense of the word. The missing ingredient is trust. According to Francis Fukuyama in *Trust,* as of 1993, 37 percent of Americans felt they could trust most people, down from 58 percent in 1960.[3] Yet human beings crave trusting relationships. The solution, of course, is that we ought to develop community amongst ourselves. And true community means interdependence not independence.

According to best-selling author Scott Peck, community first must be inclusive. This means that excluding people who are "poor or doubters or divorced or sinners or males or females or of some other race or nationality" does not make authentic community. True communities are always reaching out to extend themselves. All human differences are accepted, not excluded. (*The Different Drum*, Simon & Schuster, Inc. 1987).

Second, community requires commitment and the willingness to co-exist. This means an openness to one another's differences.

Peck emphasizes that in true community, instead of being ignored, denied, hidden or changed, human differences are *celebrated* as gifts.

Third, community can never be totalitarian; it can never even be democratic; it must be consensual. This means existing by mutual consent. This gets messy; it does not make for good order. How in the world can such a community function? I suggest a place to begin is respect – mutual respect for one another, a willingness to be tolerant for the sake of unity, togetherness and intimacy. In authentic community no one tries to correct you, scold you, humiliate you or insult you. In my experience, this attitude of tolerance can develop best out of solitude and prayer, and out of a humble recognition of one's own intolerance.

Genuine community emerges as a result of meditating on one's relationship with God, indeed developing this relationship and discovering one's own fallibility and one's own failures and weaknesses, transcended by a totally accepting love.

I believe solitude is essential for community to happen. I do not mean "saying prayers," though that may or may not help. I mean learning how to become still and listen, listen to one's heart. Often "professional pray-ers" do not know how to pray. We are so busy saying prayers we have no time to listen to our hearts. And it is mostly by listening to our hearts that we hear God. By heart, I mean the inner person – our feelings, thoughts, hopes, dreams, visions, longings, wounds, triumphs and so on. Listening to these with discernment reveals the voice of God.

And God comes gently, softly, imperceptibly. We need to be still, attentive and at home with ourselves. This is hard to do; that is why we bring the busyness of the marketplace into our place of prayer and then wonder why our lives are not being transformed. We need to practice the discipline of being alone, becoming still, and listening to our "heart." And in the perspective that emerges from this listening, we hear the "voice of God" speak to us words of encouragement and of hope. Out of solitude we can then go forth and speak words of encouragement and hope to our brothers and sisters; and so we nurture a community into a living, breathing reality of transforming intimacy, authentic care and compassion.

Social alienation can be overcome only when each one of us takes personal responsibility to form such a community in our lives. Then the fear of loneliness can be dispelled, then God's Kingdom will come to our neighborhood.

But how do we start a community? I don't think there is a single formula, technique or method. I believe one can start a community by making contact with the friends you already have, and invite them to join. Then get together on a given day for an hour or two, and pray together. See what evolves. I am sure fear will initially be present, but as you work out the defining parameters of your specific community you will be pleasantly surprised at the results.

I believe a Christian community must always be for others. I mean praying together ought to lead to a mission, to proclaim God's Kingdom to many. This entails taking on a ministerial responsibility, whether that means working in a soup kitchen, visiting the elderly in nursing homes or volunteering to drive a home-bound person to the grocery store. The joy and sense of "belonging" that these works will generate will more than compensate for your time and energy spent on the ministry.

But community is not about compensation, it is about using what talents God has given us to make God's Kingdom that much more visible on the face of this earth.

A liberating way of Jesus:
The Talents

I'll illustrate this reflection on the fears generated by loneliness by exploring the parable of the talents with you. This will show the importance of stepping forward with, instead of isolating, the gift we are to many.

> Then the Kingdom of Heaven will be like this: ... It is like a man on his way abroad who summoned his servants and entrusted his property to them. To one he gave five talents, to another, two, to a third, one; each in proportion to his ability. Then he set out. (Mt. 25:1; 14-15)

Each of us is given gifts, potentials for happiness, capacities to be loving and caring, indeed "talents" sufficient to know that we have more than we need, not only to succeed but to succeed very well in life. God has entrusted God's own wherewithal to us, and God has done so in abundance.

John Donahue observes in *The Gospel in Parable* that the issue in this parable is about faithfully maintaining a trust.[4] While the distribution of the property is unequal – five, two and one talent – the amounts involved are really enormous. One talent equals the wages of an ordinary worker for fifteen years. Entrusting so much to his servants informs us that the master has enormous trust in each one of them and confidence in their innate abilities to turn a profit for him in his absence.

When we feel socially isolated, for whatever reason, it is extremely difficult for us to grasp our immense worth. Time and time again, we all face the temptation to discount what we have. It is easy to do when we are depressed and feel rejected. I believe the challenge at those times is to review our lives and look only for the many gifts, kindnesses, loving and compassionate deeds we have done, and to give thanks to God for entrusting us with so much. It will be very helpful then to share this with another, a special friend, a spiritual director or counselor, explaining the motive to her or him why we need to share it. And the reason is to help us regain true perspective on our own self-worth.

The socially isolated person is one who has lost perspective due to a lack of or a loss of affection. It can be regained by looking within and seeing the truth: We have many good and beautiful things within us that we may have temporarily lost sight of, but that does not mean they no longer exist. Just because it may be a cloudy day, or even an overcast week, does not mean the sun has disappeared forever.

> The man who had received the five talents promptly went and traded with them and made five more. The man who had received two made two more in the same way. But the man who had received one went off and dug a hole in the ground and hid his master's money. (Mt. 25: 16-18)

Business investments, like life, involve risks. When we feel isolated and fearful of breaking out of our isolation, it requires enormous courage to take the risks that investing anew requires. I believe, though, that if we fearlessly take our own personal inventories and then reach out to another for help, we are on our way to a successful pay off. I think the trick is not to wait. The longer we wait, the more ensconced we become in our own fears and the easier it is to give in to despair.

Breaking out, investing in others, is hard to do, but if we can trust that we have what it takes, and get back into society promptly, the easier will the return be. The five- and two-talent men went for it promptly, Jesus says, and so doubled what they had. They did this knowing that what they had was a lot, but they also knew of the great trust put in them by their master; they knew they were worthwhile. This knowledge prompted them to act with alacrity and so they doubled what was entrusted to them.

This is our challenge when fears of isolation and loneliness overcome us: to believe in ourselves, to know God trusts our ability to emerge from our sorrow, and indeed to become twice or five times the person we were before the tragedy.

But many of us are tempted to act more like the one-talent man than like the other two. We bury what we have. We hide from social contacts and prefer the dark hole of isolation. This choice, of course, becomes particularly tempting when we feel alienated and alone. Taking risks is the last thing we want to do when we are in such a state. The "security" of a dark hole feels a lot safer. We actually prefer to remain hidden. We prefer isolation to community. We prefer the known misery to the effort and risk of the unknown joy.

The parable now moves into the time of reckoning, for it goes on to say:

> Now a long time afterwards, the master of those servants came back and went through his accounts with them. The man who had received the five talents came forward bringing five more. "Sir," he said, "you entrusted me with five talents; here are five more that I have made." His master said to him, "Well done, good and trustworthy servant; you have shown you are trustworthy in small things; I will trust you with greater; come and join in your master's happiness."

Next, the man with the two talents came forward. "Sir,"
he said, "you entrusted me with two talents; here are two
more that I have made." (Mt. 25: 19-22)

As with the five-talent servant before him, the master not only
commends him but rewards him extravagantly by saying:

"Well done, good and trustworthy servant; you have shown
you are trustworthy in small things. I will trust you with
greater; come and join in your master's happiness."
(Mt. 25: 23)

The irony, as we have seen, is that five and two talents are not
by any means "small things;" they represent enormous wealth.
And now, because they risked, and doubled their master's in-
come as a result, they are to be trusted with even more, and not
only that, but they will be joining the master in his own happiness.

Fidelity to ourselves, to the trust God puts in us, realizes enormous benefits. Often, I feel, we make God out to be too small,
like us, cheap in rewarding genuine fidelity. But God is not like
us. God is far more generous than we give God credit for. God
yearns, in fact, to share His/Her own happiness with us, nothing
less. And this happiness is available to us now, not only in a
future "eternal life," but now, today.

The five- and two-talent men were faithful to their trust because they knew that they would do well in their investments.
They knew the master trusted them, and because of this trust the
master was with them even while being away for a long time.
They knew they were not alone, and so they courageously risked
– and won!

But now we come to the one-talent man.

Last came forward the man who had the single talent. "Sir,"
said he, "I had heard you were a hard man, reaping
where you had not sown and gathering where you
had not scattered; so I was afraid, and I went off and
hid your talent in the ground. Here it is; it was yours,
you have it back." But his master answered him, "You
wicked and lazy servant! So you knew that I reap

> where I have not sown and gather where I have not
> scattered? Well then, you should have deposited my
> money with the bankers, and on my return I would
> have got my money back with interest. So now, take
> the talent from him and give it to the man who has the
> ten talents." (Mt. 25: 24-28)

John Donahue observes that this is the section of the parable that causes shock and surprise.[5] Actually, the third servant was not a bad person; he was just one filled with fear because of a faulty God image. There has been no evidence that the master was a hard man: Entrusting him with one whole talent hardly represents being a hard man, as we have seen. It is a lot of money. Donahue notes that entrusting so much money shows considerable magnanimity. But behind the excuse of the third servant lies this "fatal flaw," which challenges the readers to see things from the side of the master.[6] Believing in a faulty characterization of the master led the third servant to give in to his fears, and this is what eventually did him in. Acting out of fear, he did what he felt was the safest thing: He acted as little as possible. We see that fear prevents him from stepping into the unknown, as Dan Otto Via observes. He will not risk trying to fulfill his own possibilities; therefore his existence is defined in the narrowest kind of way. Action is paralyzed by anxiety. This paralysis resulted because he chose to understand himself as a victim. He refused to take a risk, and so he lost the opportunity for a rich and fulfilling life.[7] For the parable concludes:

> "As for this good-for-nothing servant, throw him
> into the darkness outside, where there will be weeping and
> grinding of teeth." (Mt. 25:30)

Actually, this last state was nothing new for this third servant. He had chosen his fate already by allowing his fears to consume him. As do we, when we allow our fears of loneliness, isolation and alienation to consume us.

So, the task at hand is to step forth courageously, trusting that God is with us, because God has already entrusted us with many talents. The task then is to take the risks necessary to step out of our little self-made holes, stop blaming others, and boldly reach out to friends, colleagues, "bankers," who will then foster for us not only dividends of joy but a new meaning and purpose for our life as well.

In this chapter I have tried to deal with the fear of loneliness. I discussed four types of loneliness that I am familiar with and tried to suggest practical ways of coping with them. Then I used the parable of the talents to illustrate the importance of recognizing the gifts we have already, and the necessity of investing them in ways that will draw us out of our cells of isolation.

Before I conclude this chapter, I feel it necessary to point out that which may be obvious to some: Loneliness is not aloneness. For me, aloneness is desirable and fulfilling. I can write only when I am alone, I pray when I am alone, I can play when I am alone, for when I am alone I don't feel at all isolated. I don't feel lonely. In fact, I feel a deep sense of community, a sense of belonging. This sense comes from within me, out of an awareness that my God is with me at these times more so even than when I am not alone – but also out of an awareness that I am in communion with many people out there in a deeply satisfying spiritual sense. Loneliness, on the other hand, as we have seen, is just the opposite, for it is a sense of isolation and abandonment. I believe our God calls us to aloneness but not to loneliness.

Believing that God is dwelling within us already, and trusting that because of this Divine indwelling we already have the power for transformation, we can boldly take the necessary steps to transcend our fear of loneliness into wellsprings of love.

In order to help initiate such a process, I invite you to use the following exercises as you see fit. Pay attention to what may well up within you while doing them, and I hope you see springs of fresh, sparkling confidence and love come forth.

The Loneliness Inventory
---

1) My age is:

2) I have felt lonely when:

3) The steps I take to alleviate my loneliness are:

4) "Home" for me means:

5) I find meaning in my life in (name the person, place or thing) because:

6) I have experienced the death of (name the person) in my life. I took the following steps to deal with my grief:

7) I have cared for (name the person) when he/she was grieving by:

8) I have experienced/not experienced the break-up of a love relationship in my life. I took the following steps to deal with the ensuing loneliness:

9) I have challenged society's idea of who I am by:

10) The consequences of my actions resulted in:

11) My understanding of an ideal community is:

12) What is the relationship between solitude and community for me?

An Exercise for The Talents (I)

List your talents.

Become still. Close your eyes. See yourself using each one of your talents in particular instances.

Allow yourself to take pride in the accomplishments your talents have generated. Delight in them; savor their fruits in your life, one by one.

Feel gratitude for your talents and accomplishments. Thank God for each one of them by name. Repeat, as in a litany, if you so wish.

An Exercise for the Talents (II)

Is there a talent you have buried out of fear or for some other reason? What steps can you take to unearth it? Are you willing to do so?

You are now told that your future happiness depends on your unearthing this one talent. How do you greet this news?

Ask yourself whether you are willing to take the practical steps necessary to unearth this one talent? Take your time about your answer.

Ask Jesus to direct your thinking in this matter. Do so by listening to your fears over unearthing your hidden talent. List them if you wish, and then allow yourself to dream over ways they can be overcome. Dreams can be eventually rendered practical if we persevere with them in companionship with God, and sometimes with God speaking through other trusted people.

Fear of Loneliness

These days my life feels a shattered crate,
splinters in every plank.

The blood oranges have rolled away,
their green-paper wrappings unfurled
on the sawdust floor.

Spiders and ants are nesting in my heart.

But often enough the wind blows.
The webs are cleared away,
and the ants scatter in all directions

because the wind blows where it will
and on it lingers the scent of the tree
that bore this fruit.

Chapter V

FEAR OF THINGS

e fear those things we cannot control.   A sense of powerlessness generates fear, and the more we fear, the more powerless we feel.   It becomes a vicious cycle that can lead to a type of paralysis.

Each of us has our own private set of things we fear, from fear of death to fear of snakes. I have already reflected on the fear of other people and the fear we all have of loneliness. In this chapter I will try to reflect on things that function outside ourselves. (Of course, insofar as the one constant in all fear is ourselves, my reference to "outside" may not be entirely accurate but I am making the distinction in the interest of clarity.)

I think we can bring these fears under control if we can understand their roots. In fact, all fears can be ameliorated to some extent if we can understand them. But understanding takes courage, and we find that even more courage is needed to overcome the understood fear because overcoming it requires changing some attitude within ourselves that has become ingrained and comfortable through force of habit. We, therefore, prefer to hang on to our fears rather than let go of them.

Yet a Christian who wants to do more than pay lip service to his or her faith must choose to let go of the fear of things, for this would be doing the work of God, on a very personal level. Jesus, after all, came to set us free from fear, and the true disciple is the one who goes forth to proclaim this message to others. This does not mean that the true disciple does not fear, but it does mean that he or she cooperates daily with God's Holy Spirit to reduce those fears to manageable levels so that they do not cripple the otherwise eager disciple.

This reducing of our fears is done, I believe, through a process in which love gradually transforms the fears into an avenue of courage. Again, it happens in solitude, in listening to God's astonishing acceptance of us. There is nothing we can do to get God to stop accepting us as we are. Once this sinks in, really sinks in, we are free, and fears consequently dissipate.

Now, having said this, I must add that I think it is very important to recognize that certain fears have a physiological base and need to be treated accordingly. Depression, anxiety, and mood disorders are real. Anxiety syndromes like panic disorders (sudden panic attacks), agoraphobia (the fear of going out in public and open spaces), obsessive-compulsive disorders (repetitive acts such as hand washing over and over again due to fear of germs), and other such disorders must be taken seriously. They can also be treated.

It is very important, I believe, to seek out a physician who is sympathetic to the distress and ask him or her for help. Many of the people I see for counseling are also seen by psychiatrists who have them on medication, including antidepressants, that helps their conditions remarkably.[1]

Aside from these diseases that have a biological base, however, there are others no less painful that cause great fear. These fears are exaggerated responses to various situations and conditions in society that we bump into. They are called *phobias* and have as a common denominator irrational rather than rational origins. Such sufferers, though, often rationalize the irrational as a way of coping with their fears. The result of this is a significant increase in stress and can often represent an overload situation in a person's life. Some examples are fear of flying, fear of heights, fear of animals, fear of driving a car, fear of school, fear of the workplace, fear of success, fear of failure, and the like. All can contribute to a stress-filled and even destructive lifestyle.

In all of these instances we find a real danger being substituted for an inner anxiety or fear. Neurotic anxiety involves using maladaptive coping techniques to deal with the tension caused by the fear. In these instances, avoidance behavior is engaged in – "I will never fly." – instead of dealing with the source of the problem, which is internal; in other words, the enemy within.

Handling fear of things

What do we do about these fears? I believe it is very important, first of all, that we not judge ourselves or condemn ourselves for having irrational fears. The fact that they may have an irrational origin does not make them any the less painful. And anyone who tries to shame us into not feeling fear – "Aw, come on, you can do it; even a kid can climb down this little cliff!" – is not helping matters at all and is being unkind. Further, while the fear or phobia may be mostly irrational, there is always a rational dimension to the fear. For example, while we know flying is by far the safest form of transportation, there *are* occasional crashes, which, of course, make sensational newspaper stories, while the far greater daily carnage on the streets does not.

Second, I think it can be very helpful to calmly look at the fear in one's solitude. This does not mean that we are to analyze it or examine it, but rather acknowledge its presence in one's life in a state of tranquility. The late Indian philosopher Krishnamurti advises: Just look at it. When fear lifts its head above the horizons of conscious thought, just look at it. Do not judge it; if you do, you make it worse. By trying to get rid of it you make it worse. Neutral observation is what he advises, for this alone can reduce considerably the effect of fear on our nerves, or even suppress it altogether. You must believe that you are greater than your fear, and hence you are capable of living with the fear without the fear consuming you.[2]

I have always had a fear of snakes. I would run; I mean, run in terror, if I came upon a snake without warning. Over the years I have forced myself to get to know snakes, to study them, to look at them closely, both in zoos and pet stores as well as in the wild. I would photograph them and look at the photos later. I consciously worked, or I should say, work at overcoming my irrational fear of snakes. I realized there was a dimension of rationality in fearing snakes, but I also knew that my behavior was often irrational, and it was this that I wanted to change. I have had many chances to test this, for where I live, snakes live, too. I have had two recent encounters with them, and in each instance I did not run. I stood and watched them, each one no more than three to four feet from me. After the initial shock, I felt no fear. When a neighbor killed them I actually felt sorrow. I think I have come a long way! Not that I like them, but that I am no longer terrified of them.

Third, I suggest that you talk out your fear with a trusted

friend, a spiritual director, a counselor, or a psychologist. This brings an objective viewpoint into the picture, and he or she may be able to help you process the fear, get it out in the open, as it were, and suggest various tools to overcome it, or at least render it manageable. These professionals can also detect whether the fear needs more help than conversation, and if so recommend a psychiatrist you could see.

One of my clients is a young man who gets panic attacks, triggered by a fear of death. They were terrible: heart palpitations, stomach problems, cold sweats, tension headaches and so on. They were so bad he had to drop out of college. He went to a hospital, was thoroughly checked out, and the doctors found nothing physiologically wrong with him. He had always been an anxious person, and in childhood would fear thunderstorms and earthquakes in a terrible way. Living on the West Coast, he had reason to fear earthquakes, but his fears were excessive, even feeling the ground moving under his feet at times when no earthquake was in progress.

He went to see a psychologist who diagnosed his condition as "general anxiety disorder with occasional panic attacks in the midst of it." The psychologist advised floating through the attack and not trying to stop it or control it. When he told me of his pain, my heart went out to him. I assured him he was a truly gifted, very talented person who sometimes felt out of control in his life. I reiterated what the psychologist told him and urged him to see the panic attacks as chances for letting go of control and letting God take over his life. I suggested he use the Jesus Prayer when the attacks came, knowing that the power of His name is greater than any perceived danger.

I also introduced him to meditation and fantasy prayer. He started taking time off to do the exercises I gave him, and over a period of time found that the affirmation he was receiving during these times of solitude was truly healing him. The number of panic attacks diminished over several months and eventually were gone altogether.

For those of us who believe in the revelations of Jesus the Christ, I believe there is a fourth action we can take to overcome our fear of things, or at least render them manageable. It has to do with the central commandment of Jesus:

...love one another,
as I have loved you.
No one can have greater love
than to lay down his life for his friends. (Jn. 15: 12-13)

Often we tend to lose sight of the potential we have for transforming ourselves through this commandment of Jesus. This is because we often prefer to keep it in the abstract and not incorporate it into our lives in a practical and personal way. Yet there is a very specific aspect to this command that can make it *the* instrument of healing for all our phobias. For it says "love one another *as I have loved you.*" And Jesus loved us by giving completely, totally, without counting the cost, without thinking of himself at all, filled with fear yet allowing the fear to be transcended by love.

St. Luke says Jesus prayed in Gethsemane thus:

"Father," he said, "if you are willing, take this cup away from me. Nevertheless, let your will be done, not mine."
(Lk. 22: 42)

Yes, Jesus was afraid, but his trust, his total trust in God, his "Abba," Father, was so complete that he surrendered his fears to God, confident in the power of that love.

And herein lies the lesson for us. Fears of things are transcended; not removed, but *transcended* – i.e. climbed over, gone beyond the limits of – by love. Only a genuine care, compassion, empathy for my brother and sister can control my fears. For a genuine care, compassion and empathy means pouring myself out for others without taking an accounting of what it will cost me.

That accounting, if taken, will always include fears of some *thing*, like the cross for Jesus. It will reveal the true power of love for we will find that we have climbed over our fear out of love for another. A way of overcoming our fear of things, therefore, is to put people first out of a warm and caring heart.

We have all read about heroes doing heroic things. But heroes are ordinary people who did what they did because they knew it was the more loving thing to do, the right thing to do, not because they lost their fear of this or that thing.

I believe it is necessary to ask ourselves whether we truly want to start a brand new life, a life free from fears, a life of peace based on understanding love developed daily in authenticity because its unfolding dimensions excite more our core than our mantle. It is strange but true that most of us prefer not to be free from fear; most of us prefer the security; we prefer the power and the prestige; we prefer the guarantees that holding on to our fears provide us. Yet it seems that following Jesus is all about letting go of fears and taking the risks that only love can take. And since God chose to become human, God has consecrated and merged the human with the divine. Hence we should take all the human means available to us to become more like God. It is but a fitting return of thanksgiving. And God is a God free from fear, a God who, having known fear, overcame it with enormous trust in the fidelity of Love.

I believe this is our challenge as well: to overcome our fears, using every human means possible, trusting implicitly in the fidelity of a God of freedom and love and so put our faith into practice in a very practical and tangible way. This means, for example, that if we fear poverty we reach out and work with the poor; if we fear displacement, we work with refugees; if we fear ridicule, we work with and for the homeless; if we fear rejection, we work with a minority; and if we fear AIDS, we work with HIV-positive patients and get to know them as sisters and brothers.

A friend of mine who was brought up in a bigoted and sexually abusive household now works with AIDS patients. She is finding such deep rewards in listening to them and counseling them in their last days on earth that she feels the fears she had initially have mostly dissipated. She feels she has replaced these fears with an understanding and love for these, the "lepers of today," that she can only describe as grace. She feels that through this work, her fear-based former life has been transformed into a new freedom in which she feels quite comfortable "moving in circles on this earth that have become rich sources of my creative expression."

Overcoming fears demands work. The extent to which we are willing to work at overcoming our fears determines how serious we are about overcoming them. Many of us talk a lot about becoming free, but it seems the more we talk – and the louder we get – the less sincere we sound. If we truly believe that God sent

Jesus, God's only Son, to save us, that means God saw we were in some way imprisoned and needed saving. Redemption, after all, is a word used in slave-holding societies, so if we use it we have to take "a fearless personal inventory," as they teach in Alcoholics Anonymous, and investigate those aspects of ourselves that are enslaved, that need redeeming. Then we can allow God to save us through prayer and solitude, other people, self-help programs, and the like. The courage that will emerge from within us as we feel "in touch" with that specific truth about ourselves will set us free. We will recognize that we are truly unique, remarkably gifted and capable of becoming sensitive, patient, caring persons free of inordinate fears because the fears have become sources of compassion.

Jesus' way: The Parable of the Sheep and the Goats

In the final parabolic discourse of Jesus in the gospel of Matthew, we find the parable of the Sheep and the Goats – the last judgment. In this allegorical presentation we find a further powerful reason to do what it takes to get over our fear of things, especially if our particular fear keeps us from reaching out to our brothers and sisters in need, and so become healed. The parable also provides a very simple way for us to overcome our fear of things, particularly *the* thing that some of us may still fear: death and the afterlife. I'll begin by introducing the foundation of the parable:

> When the Son of man comes in his glory, escorted by
> all the angels, then he will take his seat on his throne
> of glory. All nations will be assembled before him and
> he will separate people one from another as the shepherd
> separates sheep from goats. He will place the sheep on
> his right hand and the goats on his left. (Mt. 25: 31-33)

We have all seen grand depictions of the Last Judgment, with appropriate sound effects of trumpets and horns, numerous angels, and God, descending from the clouds, radiant in splendor, shimmering in an aura of golden glory. Well, as marvelous as this image may be, it has little to do with the Last Judgment as envisioned by Jesus.

What we have is something quite ordinary. Sheep and goats, mixed flocks, were fairly common in first-century Palestine and were, by definition, unruly. They would be constantly wandering off and the shepherds would have to constantly be working the herd.

This is the foundation for the parable – that of a shepherd separating his mixed herd of sheep and goats. This was really not that difficult a task. Even a young boy could tell the difference between sheep and goats and separate them with little difficulty. Scripture scholar Pheme Perkins observes that "there is none of the dramatic destruction of sinners. No book of life or computer-assisted record of each person's deeds would be required to do this job. In fact, a good sheep dog would be of considerably more help than the angelic hosts."[3]

> Then the King will say to those on his right hand, "Come, you whom my Father has blessed, take as your heritage the Kingdom prepared for you since the foundation of the world. For I was hungry and you gave me food, I was thirsty and you gave me drink, I was a stranger and you made me welcome, lacking clothes and you clothed me, sick and you visited me, in prison and you came to see me." Then the upright will say to him in reply, "Lord, when did we see you hungry and feed you, or thirsty and give you drink? When did we see you a stranger and make you welcome, lacking clothes and clothe you? When did we find you sick or in prison and go to see you?" And the King will answer, "In truth I tell you, insofar as you did this to one of the least of these brothers of mine, you did it to me." Then he will say to those on his left hand, "Go away from me, with your curse upon you, to the eternal fire prepared for the devil and his angels. For I was hungry and you never gave me food, I was thirsty and you never gave me anything to drink, I was a stranger and you never made me welcome, lacking clothes and you never clothed me, sick and in prison and you never visited me." Then it will be their turn to ask, "Lord, when did we see you hungry or thirsty, a stranger or lacking clothes, sick or in prison, and did not come to your help?" Then he will answer, "In truth I tell you, insofar as you neglected to do this to one of the least of these, you neglected to do it to me." And they will go away to eternal punishment, and the upright to eternal life. (Mt. 25: 34-46)

Most of the parable consists of the identical exchanges between the King and the two groups, and neither group seems too bright, Perkins notes.[4] They do not seem to quite recognize where they are, or what is going on, and when they are separated from each other they protest, not very sure when they succeeded or failed to succeed in these acts of love toward their neighbor. A rather dumb lot, these sheep and these goats!

The litany of deeds is repeated four times – food for the hungry, drink for the thirsty, hospitality for the stranger, clothing for the naked, aid for the sick and the imprisoned. Perkins tells us that these actions defined "love of the brethren" in early Christian communities (e.g. Rom. 12: 9-21; 15:7; Jas. 2: 14-17; 5: 14).

The surprise in this parable is the identification of the King with the outcasts of the community. Christ is hidden amongst the hungry, the thirsty, the stranger, the naked, the sick and imprisoned. This is where Christ is to be found. For when the befuddled sheep and the confused goats ask the King when did they do or not do these deeds, he says:

> "I tell you solemnly, insofar as you did this to one of
> the least of these brothers of mine, you did it to me."
> (Mt. 25:40)

Matthew ends the litany with a formal conclusion indicating this is the last word, this is what it is all about. He answers the goats' confusion by saying:

> "I tell you solemnly, insofar as you neglected to do this to
> one of the least of these, you neglected to do it to me."
> (Mt. 25:45)

He concludes by saying:

> "And they will go away to eternal punishment, and the
> virtuous to eternal life." (Mt. 25: 46)

Justice, and hence authentic Christian living, for Matthew, is a question of helping the marginalized of society. Those who actively do so are those who are doing God's will, for caring for the outcasts of society is what will make the world "right" again, according to God's plan. And if we actively care for those in need, fear of the future – among all those other things we fear – can be dissipated.

As important as justice is mercy. John Donahue points out

that "mercy," which suggests forbearance from inflicting harm or forgiveness of wrong, conceals its dynamic character. The biblical term *eleos* primarily describes an action rather than an attitude; saving help, rather than passive forbearance. Concrete actions of loving kindness to those in need constitute the mercy which God desires.[5] And becoming a merciful people can transform us from the confines our fears impose on us into signs of love on this earth.

The scene of this parable of the last judgment is apocalyptic. Apocalyptic is a view of human history not from our perspective but from God's. We have a divine vision presented to us, of how matters will turn out in the end. We have often wondered about the triumph of evil over good in our days. We need wonder no longer!

Jesus is telling us, no matter how bad things look, good will triumph in the end. If we believe this, our fears can truly no longer control us. Donahue asserts that apocalyptic affirms that the sufferings and injustice which mar this world will be bearable because the order of justice will be restored. The world will be made "right" again.[6]

In Jesus' life, death and resurrection, this apocalyptic scenario has already been inaugurated, for in Jesus *the* act of justice and mercy has been enacted. This true order of justice, though, must be enacted by us as well, and we do this in cooperation with Jesus when we step out of our isolation, transcend our fears by choosing to love, and reach out to the least of our sisters and brothers with concrete acts of mercy.

Inherent in the Last Judgment, of course, is a warning. Those of us who believe that going to church regularly and fulfilling the rituals of our religion suffices to "guarantee" for us eternal life, had better think again! The parable says that what counts us among God's blessed are acts – concrete acts – of compassion towards those people in our specific society whom we rather not acknowledge, let alone allow into our circle of friends. Much "church work" and public worship counts for very little if there is no time and energy set aside for the downtrodden among us. Church must be church *in mission*, which, through its teaching and way of life, gives witness to Jesus. This community we call church does so not by simply indicting an evil world but by being a light to the world so that people will give glory to God, Donahue emphasizes.[7]

The fearful amongst us must be reminded that fear of things, no matter what these "things" may be, need not shape our lives forever. We also have a promise from God that climbing over our current fears through concrete acts of compassion will include us among God's blessed. We have the power within us to fashion our own future, our destiny. This power belongs to no one else but us, and we know what we have to do to break out of our fearful cells and become beacons of hope, lights to those who live in darkness.

Merciful care, helping the poor, reaching out to the homeless and so on is what true religion is all about. Of course, this has previously been illustrated over and over again as we have seen in such parables as the Good Samaritan, the Prodigal Son, the Widow and the Judge, the Talents, and so many others. But in this final parable of Matthew, it is spelled out for us in a quite unambiguous way. True religion, true worship, true faith, true spirituality is lived out in works of mercy and compassion for the weakest, the least worthy of society.

It must be noted that God does not do the judging. The sheep are sheep before the judgment; the goats are goats already. God only does the *sorting*; God simply *ratifies* our decision.

A further point of considerable importance, especially for those of us who live in fear, is that God makes it very clear that doing these deeds of loving kindness to the least in our society makes us members of the blessed, not in the dim future, but *right now*, today. What a marvelous guarantee, one that if truly believed and understood – not just with our minds but with our hearts as well – can melt all the fears we may have. What we do is love, concretely, tangibly, that brother or sister we may not particularly recognize as such, and we are loving God. And this reaching out will eliminate all fears about our future dwelling place: It will be with God, for it is with God today for those of us who love God by loving our neighbor.

Much of our anxiety and many of our fears can be significantly reduced if today we decide to help ourselves by helping a family in need, a fearful neighbor, a motorist broken down on the side of the road, a terrified child afraid of his or her parent.

Nelson Mandela, in his 1994 Inaugural speech, challenged all of us when he said:

> Our deepest fear is not that we are inadequate. Our deepest fear is that we are powerful beyond measure. It is our light, not our darkness, that most frightens us. We ask ourselves, who am I to be brilliant, gorgeous, talented and fabulous? Actually, who are you not to be? You are a child of God. Your playing small doesn't serve the world. There's nothing enlightened about shrinking so that other people won't feel insecure around you. We were born to make manifest the glory of God that is within us. It's not just in some of us; it's in everyone. And as we let our own light shine, we unconsciously give other people permission to do the same. As we are liberated from our fear, our presence automatically liberates others.

I believe taking these words to heart can help to transform us from being a fearful people into images of God. Then, as Teilard de Chardin, the late paleontologist and Jesuit, once said, "For the second time on the face of this earth, humankind would have discovered fire."

Let us turn to some exercises now as a way of interiorizing these words. In this instance, though, the palliative for healing our fear of things will lead us from an initial interiorizing outward, toward our sisters and brothers in need. And so we become healed.

The Fear of Things Inventory

1) The things I fear include the following:

2) I want to/do not want to change my fear because:

3) In order to become free of this fear, I am willing to:

4) I will allow (person, process or spiritual being) to help me overcome this fear.

5) I have seen a mental health professional for my fears of:
   He/she prescribed:
   It helped/did not help me because:

6) I have a phobia for:

7) I have used the following coping techniques to help me deal with my neurosis/neuroses:

8) I am open to meditative techniques as a way of helping me deal with my fears because I believe:

9) I believe God cares about my irrational fears because:

Fear of Things
(A poem for meditation)

A beast approaches.
It is wearing a mask.
I fear it because
I cannot see its
true face.

Yet if I could see
its true face, why
would I fear?

What is my deepest fear?

Am I afraid
because I do not
know?

An Exercise for the Parable of the Sheep and the Goats

This is a practical exercise.

Resolve in prayer to reach out, in whatever creative way you can, to a person or persons you may have little or no contact with on a regular basis, beginning today.

These people could be the following:
- Your parents
- Your children
- The lonely in a nursing home
- Prisoners
- The homeless
- The sick
- Others (Add your own options to this list.)

Ask yourself what you can specifically do to help them.

(I promise you, your life will become immeasurably enriched, and your fears will dissipate the more you become involved with them.)

Conclusion

*F*ears are not overcome; they are *transcended by love.* The person who boldly faces the unknown, who reaches out to the stranger in need or the social outcast, is not someone devoid of fear but someone who has found courage in the face of fear because he or she has found love.

Robert Furey, in his fine book *Facing Fear: The Search for Courage,* observes wisely, "Courage doesn't make things easier. It makes things possible!"[1] We do what we have to do because it is the right thing to do, not because we have suddenly lost our fears and found courage. The person who faces a grave danger without any fear is an idiot. Fear protects us from danger. However, irrational fears that keep us from living life to the fullest can cripple us and so prevent us from taking the calculated risks that living as a daughter or son of God requires.

Faith means taking risks. We will truly live out our faith only if we feel the risks are worth taking – only if we feel God is worth our trust. That is why redefining our God image is so crucial. No matter what we say, it is exceedingly difficult to trust a God who we perceive to be punitive, or threatening, a manipulator or a kill-joy. Rather, we tend more to trust a God who is love; to the extent that we do not trust God to be love, to that extent we have yet to interiorize the words of St. John when he said quite plainly:

> God is love,
> and anyone who lives in love lives in God,
> and God lives in him. (1 Jn. 4:16)

We go about interiorizing these moving words by boldly looking deeply into our fears, identifying their sources, and – with much trust and confidence in the words of sacred scripture – replacing each of our fears with love. In this way we can, little by little, realize God's hope for us, that we live in love, and so allow our entire lives to be transformed by the realization that living in love means living in God. Then God will be dwelling in us, and all our fears will evaporate. For we will then know:

> In love there can be no fear,
> but fear is driven out by perfect love.... (1 Jn. 4:18)

It is essential that we be patient with ourselves in this process, remembering the old story of the tourist in New York City who asked the taxi driver how to get to Carnegie Hall. His answer: "Practice, practice, practice!"

Practice means understanding; the more the musician practices, the more he or she understands the composer's intent, the composer's heart and soul. And the more the musician understands the composer's heart and soul, the more the music soars and reflects the composer's vision. Likewise, the more we practice replacing our fears with love, the more we will reflect The Great Composer's heart and soul, The Great Composer's Vision.

In this book I have tried to deal with various aspects of fear and suggest that a way out of them is through re-encountering the teachings of Jesus, as illustrated in his parables. I believe that if we truly listen to the voice of Jesus speak to us through them we will find that Jesus can truly become our liberator in a very tangible and personal way. This freedom can be ours if we open our minds and hearts to His teachings and be willing to take the practical steps necessary to accomplish it.

These practical steps, I repeat, *involve discipline.* First, the discipline of seeking and finding time for solitude in our lives. During this time we can perhaps use the exercises and scripture found in this book to alter our faulty God images and take an inventory of the landscape of fears in our life. Then, or concomitantly, we can seek and find a kind and compassionate spiritual director, counselor, therapist, priest or minister to help us overcome our fears through talking them out and perhaps sharing the results of our inventories. This could objectify them to the point of rendering our fears non-toxic to us. Thirdly, we can act to overcome our fears in a practical way by choosing to love a less fortunate sister or brother in concrete and tangible ways on a regular basis.

Authors often write books not only for others but also for

themselves, to try to make sense of some difficulty they are encountering in their lives. This book is no exception. I have put into practice what I have written here, and for me, it has worked. I pray sincerely it works for you as well.

As stated earlier, fear is overcome by climbing over it out of love. Doing so, of course, also gives us the meaning of our existence. All great teachers, philosophers and founders of religions have told us so: Loving our neighbor, and especially our less fortunate neighbor, is the meaning that fulfills our life. It also liberates the fearful amongst us from the prisons and the dungeons of our own making, so that a new day dawns, one bright with freshly opened flowers, with rays of sun-ignited hope, and a consequent emerging joy from deep within our hearts.

> *To you, my sisters and brothers in faith,*
>
> *wherever you are...*
>
> *I wish you courage and peace*
>
> *as you continue on your journey...*

Bibliography

Chapter One

Kung, Hans. *On Being A Christian.* New York: Doubleday & Co., 1976

Bailey, Kenneth. *Poet & Peasant* and *Through Peasant Eyes.* Grand Rapids, Mich.: Wm. B. Eerdmans Publishing Co., 1983

Derrett, J.D.M. *Law in the New Testament.* London: Darton, Longman, & Todd, 1970.

Jeremias, Joachim. *The Parables of Jesus,* 2nd Revised Edition. New York: Charles Scribner's Sons, 1972.

Donahue, John. *The Gospel in Parable.* Philadelphia: Fortress Press, 1988.

Chapter Two

Stein, Edward V. *Guilt: Theory and Therapy.* Philadelphia: The Westminster Press, 1968.

Bradshaw, John. *Healing the Shame That Binds You.* Deerfield Beach, Fla.: Health Communications, Inc., 1988.

Fowler, James. *Stages of Faith.* San Francisco: Harper & Row, 1981.

Martos, Joseph. *Doors to the Sacred.* New York: Doubleday & Co., 1981.

deMello, Anthony. *The Song of the Bird.* India: Gujarat Sahitya Prakesh, 1982.

Via, Dan Otto, Jr., *The Parables: Their Literary and Existential Dimension.* Philadelphia: Fortress Press, 1984.

Chapter Three

Allport, Gordon W. *The Nature of Prejudice.* Reading, Mass.: Addison Wesley, 1980 (1954).

Freud, Sigmund. *Civilization and its Discontents.* New York: W.W. Norton & Co., 1961 (1930).

deMello, Anthony. *Taking Flight.* New York: Doubleday, 1988.

Argyle, M. & Beit-Hallahmi, B. *The Social Psychology of Religion.* London & Boston: Routledge & Kegan Paul, 1975.

Vachss, Andrew. "You Carry the Cure in Your Own Heart." *Parade,* Aug 28, 1994.

Chapter Four

Eliot, T.S. "The Hollow Men." *Immortal Poems of the English Language.* New York: Washington Square Press, Inc. 1965 (1952).

Wright, Robert. "The Evolution of Despair." *Time.* August 28, 1995.

Chapter Five

Dowling, Colette. *You Mean I Don't Have to Feel This Way?* New York: Bantam Books, 1993.

Valles, Carlos G. *Let Go of Fear.* Ligouri, Mo.: Triumph Books, 1993.

Perkins, Pheme. *Hearing the Parables of Jesus.* New York: Paulist Press, 1981.

Conclusion

Furey, Robert. *Facing Fear: The Search for Courage.* New York: Alba House, 1990.

References

Chapter 1

1. Hans Kung, *On Being A Christian*, (New York: Doubleday & Company, 1976), 251.

2. I suggested he reflect on Isaiah 43:1-4; Isaiah 41:8-13; Jeremiah 29:11-14; Leviticus 26:11-13; among others, as well as from the New Testament, Matthew 11:28-30; Luke 12:22-32; John 14:1-7; Mark 4:35-41.

3. Kenneth Bailey, *Poet & Peasant* and *Through Peasant Eyes*, (Grand Rapids, Mich.: Wm. B. Eerdmans Pub. Co., 1983), 43-44.

4. J.D.M. Derrett, *Law in the New Testament*, (London: 1970), 212.

5. Bailey, 46.

6. Joachim Jeremias, *The Parables of Jesus*, (New York: Charles Scribner's Sons, 1972 (1954)), 203.

7. Dr. David Duncombe, PhD, pointed out to me that the splanchnic nerve enervates both the small and large intestine, and Dr. Larry Russell, MD, informed me that the splanchnic nerve has nothing to do with higher intellect. It is completely divorced from the brain. Compassion does not make sense; in other words, it is illogical.

8. John Donahue, *The Gospel in Parable*, (Philadelphia: Fortress Press, 1988), 132.

9. J.D.M. Derrett, *Law in the New Testament*, (London: 1970), 220.

10. Bailey, 51-52.

Chapter 2

1. Edward V. Stein, *Guilt: Theory and Therapy*, (Philadelphia: The Westminster Press, 1968), 26.

2. Ibid., 166.

3. John Bradshaw, *Healing the Shame that Binds You*, (Deerfield Beach, Florida: Health Communications, Inc. 1988).

4. James Fowler, *Stages of Faith*, (San Francisco: Harper & Row, 1981), 151-173. According to Fowler, there is a pre-stage and then there are six stages of faith developmentally related. The **pre-stage** (up to about age 2), called Undifferentiated faith, combines the initial feelings of trust, courage, hope and love with sensed threats of abandonment and deprivation in an infant's environment. The inchoate faith here is between a basic trust and a failed mutuality. **Stage One**, Intuitive-Projective Faith (2-7 years), consists of the birth of the imagination. Images and symbols aided by fairy tales can powerfully symbolize inner terrors but also provide tangible models of virtue and courage. **Stage Two**, Mythic-Literal Faith (adolescence of any age), represents the stage in which the ability to bind our experiences into meaning through stories takes place. They do not, however, reflect and conceptualize the meaning of the stories. They are taken literally. Most fundamentalists prefer this stage. **Stage Three**, Synthetic-Conventional Faith, is the conformist stage. It is acutely tuned to the expectations and judgments of significant others. Authority is here located in traditional authority figures and not in its own identity and autonomy. For many adults, this is the stage they live in. **Stage Four**, Individuative-Reflective Faith, faces unavoidable tensions between individuality versus being defined by a group. It sustains its own identity by composing a meaning frame of *itself* as a "world view". It is a demythologizing stage. **Stage Five**, Conjunctive Faith, accepts truth as multidimensional since it sees things organically related to each other. It sees all sides of an issue simultaneously. It is open to another's truth. It involves a critical recognition of one's "deeper self" in which the myths, prejudices and ideal images built deeply into the self by one's social class, religious traditions, ethnic group, etc. is critically appraised. It gives rise to the irenic imagination in which the capacity to

be in one's group while seeing the relativity of its distorting apprehensions of reality occurs. **Stage Six**, Universalizing Faith, is exceedingly rare. A felt sense of an ultimate environment is inclusive of all-being. Universalizers are experienced as subversive of the structures by which we sustain our individual and corporate survival security. Many die at the hands of those they are trying to change. Inclusiveness of community, a radical commitment to justice and love, a selfless passion for a transformed world made not in their image but in accordance with a divine and transcendent reality are its characteristics.

5. Stein, 166.

6. Joseph Martos, *Doors to the Sacred*, (New York: Doubleday & Co., 1981), 315.

7. Bailey, 161-164.

8. Anthony deMello, *The Song of the Bird*, (India: Gujarat Sahitya Prakash, 1982), 200-201.

9. Jeremias, 129.

10. Bailey, 176. According to Oesterley, notes Bailey, there were three levels of servants in first century Palestine. The first were bondsmen who as slaves were part of the estate and almost part of the family; then there were slaves of a lower class, subordinate to the bondsmen; and finally the hired servants who were outsiders. The younger son proposes to himself a relationship with his father then that would keep him an outsider.

11. Jeremias, 130.

12. Dan Otto Via, Jr., *The Parables: Their Literary and Existential Dimension*, (Philadelphia: Fortress Press, 1984), 171.

13. Ibid., 166.

14. Bailey, 193-194.

Chapter 3

1. Gordon W. Allport, *The Nature of Prejudice*, (Reading, Mass.: Addison Wesley, 1980 (1954)) is my source for some of the material that follows.

2. Ibid., 6, 9.

3. Sigmund Freud, *Civilization and its Discontents*, (New York: W.W. Norton & Co., 1961)

4. Allport., 354.

5. Anthony deMello, *Taking Flight*, (NY: Doubleday, 1988), 186.

6. Michael Argyle and Benjamin Beit-Hallahmi, *The Social Psychology of Religion*, (London & Boston: Routledge & Kegan Paul, 1975), Chapter 7, among several other sources.

7. Allport, 451.

8. Andrew Vachss, "You Carry the Cure in Your Own Heart," *Parade*, Aug. 28, 1994

9. Bailey, 133.

10. Jeremias, 153.

11. Bailey, 136.

Chapter 4

1. T.S. Eliot, 'The Hollow Men,' in *Immortal Poems of the English Language*, (NY: Washington Square Press, Inc., 1965 (1952)), 539.

2. Robert Wright, "The Evolution of Despair," *Time*, August 28, 1995, 50f.

3. Ibid., 56.

4. John Donahue, *The Gospel in Parable*, (Philadelphia: Fortress Press, 1988), 106.

5. Ibid., 107.

6. Ibid., 107.

7. Via, 118-120.

Chapter 5

1. Colette Dowling, *You Mean I Don't Have to Feel This Way?* (NY: Bantam Books, 1993), in Foreword xiii-xvi.

2. Carlos G. Valles, *Let Go of Fear*, (Ligouri, Mo.: Triumph Books, 1993), 215.

3. Pheme Perkins, *Hearing the Parables of Jesus*, (New York: Paulist Press, 1981), 159.

4. Ibid., 160.

5. Donahue, 119.

6. Ibid., 119.

7. Ibid., 123.

Conclusion

1. Robert Furey, *Facing Fear: The Search for Courage*, (New York: Alba House, 1990), 8.

-Index-

About the Author...

FRANCIS W. VANDERWALL is a retreat leader, spiritual director and counselor in private practice in Lafayette, Louisiana.

A former Jesuit, he has for many years been a facilitator and leader of workshops on liturgy, ecclesial ministries, prayer, spirituality and behavior modification.

He has a doctoral degree in the Psychology of Religion from the Graduate Theological Union in Berkeley, California, as well as a masters of divinity in Theology and the Fine Arts from the Jesuit School of Theology in Berkeley.

He has written and had published several books, including *Water in the Wilderness: Paths of Prayer, Springs for Life* (1985), *Spiritual Direction: An Invitation to Abundant Life* (1981), and *Freedom From Fear: A Way Through the Ways of Jesus the Christ* (1999).